Change in
British Society

OPUS General Editors

Keith Thomas *Humanities*
J. S. Weiner *Sciences*

A. H. Halsey

Change in British Society

Based on the
Reith Lectures

1978

Oxford University Press

OXFORD MELBOURNE NEW YORK

Oxford University Press, Walton Street, Oxford OX2 6DP

OXFORD LONDON GLASGOW
NEW YORK TORONTO MELBOURNE WELLINGTON
KUALA LUMPUR SINGAPORE JAKARTA HONG KONG TOKYO
DELHI BOMBAY CALCUTTA MADRAS KARACHI
IBADAN NAIROBI DAR ES SALAAM CAPE TOWN

British Library Cataloguing in Publication Data

Halsey, Albert Henry
    Change in British society. — (Opus).
    1. Great Britain — Social conditions — 20th century
    I. Title   II. Series
    301.29'41   HN385

    ISBN 0-19-219132-2
    ISBN 0-19-289119-7 Pbk

*Set by Hope Services, Wantage
and printed in Great Britain by
Billing & Sons Ltd., Guildford and Worcester*

For Norman Dennis
True friend and exemplary citizen

Preface

THIS book on the changing face of British society is based on my Reith Lectures and on three 'Personal View' talks. In writing it, I have taken the opportunity of extending the discussion and of addressing myself to readers rather than to listeners.

For me, as no doubt for my twenty-nine distinguished predecessors, the B.B.C. lectures posed two dilemmas. Their primary purpose, and an opportunity which I welcomed and feared, was to broadcast from a chosen corner of the academic world to the wide and varied audience of those who listen to Radio 4 and Radio 3. The 'intelligent layman' is a phrase commonly used to describe them but one over which I hesitated, partly because of its faint aroma of patronage, but more because of its implicit identification of a person. In fact there is no such person. One is talking to an immense range of people with little in common other than, presumably, the capacity to understand the English language. So the first dilemma is to decide whom to talk to. There is a temptation to see one's academic colleagues behind the rather lonely and forbidding microphone into which one speaks. It stares back unblinking, offering none of those 'non-verbal responses' on which one relies in direct conversation. Yet one knows that the professionals are there, mostly friendly but untrue to their calling if not also critical. Alternatively there is that elusive falsification, the school teacher in Uttoxeter, innocent of social science but quick to detect logical error, empirical misdescription, or expository unclarity. I did my best to choose the latter audience and was firmly encouraged to do so by a benign

but sternly patient producer, George Fischer. He helped
more than he realised, for in the end I really talked to *him*,
the personification of an attentive audience, combining
unfailing goodwill with critical appreciation.

The other dilemma is that spoken English has an internal
logic and rhythm which is quite different from written
English. So what does one do about the book? I have started
again, discarding spoken for written prose wherever it
seemed necessary. More important, I have used the opportunity to escape the constraint of half-hour talks by expanding (or, more accurately, re-inserting) the written arguments.
The book also offers escape from another limitation of
sound broadcasting, enabling me to add such graphs and
statistical tables as are needed to strengthen the argument.
Moreover, I have added a chapter on mobility and education—a topic I would have included in the lectures had there
been seven rather than the traditional six.

The result is intended to provide students of all ages with
a short but comprehensive introduction to the information
needed in order to form a view of the direction of twentieth-
century social history in Britain, and to offer a sociological
interpretation of that history. In a short concluding chapter
I have deliberately trespassed beyond sociology to a moral
and political interpretation. This I have done mainly in the
hope that the reader may thereby be helped and encouraged
to form his own view and to appreciate both the separation
and the link between the social sciences and social action.

Many colleagues and friends have helped me in one way
or another in preparing the talks and the book. They include Colin Crouch, Alan Fox, John Goldthorpe, Clyde
Mitchell, Michael Teitelbaum, and Keith Thomas, the
humanities editor of this series. Margaret Bett has given me
her superb secretarial support. Above all I want to salute
Norman Dennis, whose intellectual comradeship has been
a constant delight to me over the years.

Nuffield College   A. H. HALSEY
Oxford
March 1978

Contents

List of figures

List of tables

Acknowledgements

My thanks are due to the *Oxford Review of Education* for allowing me to incorporate part of my article 'Authority, Bureaucracy, and Education' from Vol. 3, No. 3, 1977; to Routledge and Kegan Paul for allowing me to use a table from M. Young and P. Willmott, *The Symmetrical Family*; and to H.M.S.O. for allowing me to use tables from the Royal Commission on the Distribution of Income and Wealth.

1 To know ourselves

WHO are you? Where do you come from, and where are you going? These are old questions, but perhaps never before so anxiously asked, or so uncertainly answered. Each one of us knows them as personal questions: but they can also be put collectively. I want to do that in this book: to turn them, in other words, into sociological questions. To manage their immensity I want to circumscribe them in space and time: in space by concentrating on one country—Britain; in time by confining the discussion largely to the experience collectively undergone by those who live in Britain now. This will give us material enough, to demand explanation. Some Britons belong to the two-and-a-half million compatriots who are over 75, and even to the half million who are over 85—people who remember Queen Victoria and a world without radio or plastics or the Labour Party. Others belong to the 15-19 year-old age group of four million, for whom the *pax Britannica* is as remote as the *pax Romana,* whose world is post-Suez, who never rode a tram, nor wore a Sunday suit.

However, we must not infer from generational contrasts that all we need to explain is change. Continuity is no less striking and equally problematic. Each successive age group, in its distinctive collective consciousness, reflects a new world. But it also carries the past into the future. It is not only that Irishmen perennially re-fight the Battle of the Boyne, or that the B.B.C. annually re-enacts the Second World War. Adherence to ancient custom is so tenacious that at Downham Market in Norfolk, British Catholics in the 1970s have defied the modernising tendencies of the

Vatican by persisting in the celebration of the Tridentine Mass, the old Latin Mass promulgated by the Council of Trent in 1570, which was ruthlessly forbidden in the reign of the first Elizabeth.

Continuity is no accident. Social customs, like personal habit, economize human effort. They store knowledge, pre-arrange decisions, save us the trouble of weighing every choice afresh. In this way the world is ordered; but, in the same way, control in the interests of the *status quo* is more or less powerfully embodied in any society. Maintenance of that control then depends on a stable environment of which one important element is external security. In this respect British history is distinctive by contrast with the history of the European continent. The towns and villages of the island have peaceable traditions over many centuries. The last battle on British soil took place at Culloden in 1746; every other European country has known violent and bitter warfare with foreigners on its own territory. Britain has exported its bloodshed. But above all, continuity is a matter of social control and this brings with it its puzzles. For example, many have noted and praised Britain as a land of tolerance and liberty, while at the same time wondering at its capacity to resist the claims of egalitarian movements without resort to overt force.

How, then, are we to make sense of the complex amalgam of persistence and change? My answers will be those of a sociologist. This you may immediately find an imprisonment of method, especially if I add that just by living and learning to the point of reading this book, you already know practically all the sociology that is to be known. But that is a misleading truth—a play on the verb 'to know'. Sixth-form boys and girls setting out on an 'A' level science course are frequently told that they already know 95 per cent of all known physics. It is true: but the other 5 per cent transforms the meaning and the power of knowing.

What, then, are sociological questions and answers? If I again put my first question to a native of our chosen country—'Who are you?'—he or she might reply with the title of one of Graham Greene's entertainments, *England*

Made Me. The sociologist would then ask, 'How?'. Or he might quote Sir Harry Smith's mother who took leave of him saying 'If you ever meet your enemy, remember you are born a true Englishman'.[1] The sociologist would want to ask who, apart from a traditional matriarch, advances a definition of the true Englishman, what other definitions are available, from whom, and who knows them, follows them, or defies them. Sociology is about social relations—relations of individuals and groups in work and in play, war and peace, transient encounters and enduring bonds. Sociologists seek regularity and pattern in these relations. Hence they summarize them in abstractions as relations of production and reproduction, of kinship and affinity, of authority and freedom, power and advantage. They assume that the social world is not a universe of random changes and exchanges but, on the contrary, that the successful study of social relations will yield general rules governing their persistence and their rupture—rules which are by no means necessarily known to the social actors themselves.

Now I realize I have already taken us into deep water. To go further would be to navigate those oceans in which are to be found the question of free will, and whether there are laws of social motion, historical necessities, propelling us towards a determined fate. Enough. Let us defer these questions and, for the moment, contrive to imagine ourselves as visitors from some other planet, as Martian anthropologists, possessed of belief in science and of the intelligence to use it, but without the understanding which enables us to interpret our neighbour through the fact of our own humanity. What would the inter-planetary visitor see? Even without human understanding, his computer picture would reveal order rather than chaos, regularity rather than randomness. A guarded boundary of British society would be as clear to him as the physical coastline. He would notice that there are two ways of entering this society, either through the wombs of mothers and the records of the Registrar of Births, Marriages, and Deaths, or from other countries overseas and via the desk of the immigration officer. Exit is similarly marked and rule-bound.

Births, deaths, and migrations are governed not only by physical laws, but also by social mechanisms: there are both legitimate and illegitimate births and deaths. Further inspection, again unaided by any kind of human empathy, would reveal patterns and continuities of relations inside the boundary. Our Martian would quickly conceptualize pair-bonding in what we call marriage, courtship, and friendship, class structure in the social relations of production, scientific organizations in the social relations of discovery, status systems in the relations of dominance and submission, and so on. Without doubt, considerable inhuman sense could be made of British society and its history.

But our own social knowledge is both less and more than Martian. Less, because human involvement makes us creatures of our time and place, hampering us with preconceptions and prejudices, and restricting the range of our imagination. More, and it is a crucial more, because we can turn understanding to the service of scholarship. You might, therefore, think of the social sciences as striving simultaneously both to understand so as to interpret human activity, and also to achieve Martian objectivity so as to remove from it adulterating passion. This, at all events, is the intellectual posture I will adopt in my attempt to interpret recent generations of British social experience.

This is a considerable task. A single book could not hope to reproduce more than the most minute fraction of the social action and perception of a single hour in British society. Moreover, the fact that to understand other human beings is an indispensable tool to sociological explanation also constitutes a peculiar handicap in exposition because it makes sociologists of us all. Words like 'class' or 'status' are common to 'folk sociology' as well as to professional sociology, but their meanings differ (and, in the case of this particular pair of words, are usually reversed as between a newspaper and a learned article). Hence the struggle to rescue scholarship and science from gossip, which the physicist has largely won, is much harder for the social scientist, for the paradoxical reason that he more readily 'knows' and is known to the 'object' of his study.

The posture I have described as proper to sociologists, its difficulty apart, is not the only possible one for understanding society; nor is it either confined to or always adopted by sociologists. Much of our collective self-knowledge comes from fiction or books and essays in persuasion. It is arguable whether we learn more about the social circumstances of childhood at the beginning of the present century from Arthur Morrison's *A Child of the Jago,* or from Charles Booth's *London Survey* of that time. Yet there can be no doubt that accuracy of perspective is more likely to be obtained by use of the sociological method. The novel seeks drama before balance. As it happens, both of the works cited are excellent examples of their genre. But the Jago was the worst of slums, and therefore Morrison's novel tells us about childhood in that environment only, while Booth's Survey not only described but quantified the population living in a much wider range of environments. From him we receive a quantified description not only of the 'lowest class of occasional labourers, loafers and semi-criminals', but also of 'the very poor' and 'the poor', those on 'regular standard earnings', 'higher-class labour', and so on. Booth estimated the lowest class to number 11,000 out of 900,000. But this was the class, the lumpen proletariat so heartily detested by Marx, which has constantly attracted the attention and caught the imagination of research workers, reformer, and journalists. The resulting descriptions make good copy, but they tempt romantic minds to identify the working class as a whole with a distinctive and unrepresentative segment of it.

The search for objectivity through social science has another characteristic feature. Sociology, as I have said, is essentially a set of propositions about social relations, about characteristic tendencies and variations in social conditions and social consciousness. Sociological reference is thus to the role, not to the person. Even references to groups should normally be taken as statements about a structure of relations rather than an aggregate of people. For example, if we speak of the British working class, it is more often than not misleading to take this to mean a summary label for the enumeration of men and women in manual employment in Britain at a point of time. So the young sociologist Colin Crouch is faithful to his calling when he begins a book with a firm reminder to the reader that 'class is treated here as an analytical relationship rather than as the identification of empirical groups of persons'. And he goes on to point out that where this usage is carried to its logical conclusion, as in the writings of Marxists like Poulantzas, human beings are seen 'as simply the "bearers" of structural variables'.[2] At first reading, this may seem a weird distortion of language. Certainly it runs risks. It can lead to what is called the over-socialized conception of man which, in its crude form, portrays people as mere social puppets so that the Britons we study in this book are depicted as nothing but the expression of, say, bureau-cratization, or class conflict, or secularization. But the method is justified precisely to distinguish and analyse such social forces. That is what sociology is. It does not set out to describe and explain some total 'human condition'. It narrows the beam to intensify the light: and the world it thus illuminates is far from being the whole world.

What, then, can we gain from this sociological perspec-tive? Broadly, I hope, two things: we shall discern the forces of continuity and change, and we shall arrive at a clearer view of what makes for consensus and conflict in British society. As to continuity and change, we must appreciate that the country experienced by its present inhabitants was made and continues to be modified for them by forces beyond their own encounters—by its geology, topography, latitude and longitude, and by the activity of their ances-tors, labouring incessantly down the ages to master their environment. The unfinished result is their cultural inheri-tance. Whether they see it as a 'green and pleasant land', or as the cradle of 'dark, satanic mills', or both, what they see and, indeed, how they learn to see it, is rooted in a long process of human history and cultural evolution.

Much of all this we must simply take for granted, appeal-ing to what every mythical schoolboy knows, for example, that the Phoenicians dug tin in the mines of Cornwall, that

Derby, given its name, must have been founded by the Danes, or that 30.8 per cent of the inhabitants of Wales were Welsh-speaking in 1921. The lessons of history are no doubt numberless but, quite apart from sifting them out of the lessons of historians, they do not foreclose the future. A story about Scotland can illustrate both points. Edward Gibbon, writing in the eighteenth century, noted that the Romans failed to conquer northern Scotland.

The native Caledonians preserved in the northern extremity of the island their wild independence, for which they were not less indebted to their poverty than to their valour. Their incursions were frequently repelled and chastised; but their country was never subdued. The masters of the fairest and most wealthy climates of the globe turned with contempt from gloomy hills assailed by the winter tempest, from lakes concealed in a blue mist, and from cold and lonely heaths, over which the deer of the forest were chased by a troop of naked Barbarians.[3]

If we are listening here to a faithful echo of the Roman voice, we are bound to remark that the Romans could not have anticipated Gibbon's Scottish contemporaries like David Hume, or John Millar,[4] or Adam Smith,[5] who made their universities the leading centres of European thought in their day; and, if we are listening to Gibbon's amiable prejudices, we can at least remark that he could not have anticipated North Sea oil.

When sociologists or historians consider continuity and change they must also start from the commonplace generalization that man is to be distinguished from the brutes, not so much by his desire for a better life as by the range of his conception of what that life might be, and the complexity of the language in which he is able to express his hope. Our period in the twentieth century can be thought of as one of unprecedented advance in the capacity of mankind to realize dreams—at least in that one-third of the world to which Britain belongs where, in the past generation, the natural sciences have been harnessed to spectacular new dominance over nature. The power of productive systems, whether for peace or war, has transformed the significance of the age-old debate over the ends towards which society may be directed. Such clichés of political discussion as 'the revolution of rising expectations' point to that significance. Dreams have come to earth and ends are secularized. An aerial view of the island shows the motorway and the church spire as the ubiquitous monuments of human aspiration. But the spires point to other-worldly vision, and were built over centuries of a passing civilization in which the attainment of bliss was seen to belong to the next world. The road, by contrast, seems to hold out the promise of satisfaction, tomorrow if not to-day, but *on this earth* as it busily connects factory to town to suburb to coastal resort. So, for example, in the older world, poverty was accepted as inevitable, and morality was addressed to the endurance of it and its relief. In the twentieth century, the moral objective has switched from endurance to protest, and from relief to abolition. Equality is to be realized among men, not only found before God. Liberty is for the lords of the earth, not the angels in heaven.

There are, of course, those who prophesy that these dreams come true will shortly turn into living nightmares. The twentieth century in Britain and throughout the so-called first and second worlds of industrial capitalism and communism, is thought by some critics to be an interlude of materialist fantasy. The earthly paradise is a miasma and the modern secular '-isms' doomed to fail. So Mr. Mugger-idge, with a journalist's genius for self-caricature, expresses the traditionalist opposition to modernity when he tells us that if he were Pope he would form an underground church, organized to survive through the new Dark Ages we are about to enter, until the time when the world can again be given the eternal verities hitherto preserved, albeit imperfectly and with gross infidelity, by the Catholic Church.[6]

So ends remain in question and this must not be forgotten even though my purpose in this book is to consider means, that is, the changes in social organization of the past fifty years through which people in Britain have co-operated and argued in pursuit of their interests. Sociology cannot prescribe ends, but it can help us to argue about them more intelligently by describing accurately the social conditions under which people act, and the intended and unintended consequences of their actions.

Older studies of continuity, and particularly the study of national character by cultural anthropologists and historians, were posited essentially on the existence of a modal personality in each nation. The last such anthropological book on Britain (actually more narrowly focused on England) was Geoffrey Gorer's *Exploring English Character* (1953). Such works are out of fashion now: but one of them is especially remarkable. Writing as a German for Germans, Wilhelm Dibelius tell us that he conceived of his book on *England* during the First World War out of an 'overwhelming sense of a people giving its best in fighting an enemy which it did not know'.[7] He wrote in a spirit of high European liberalism, and evoked the essential manners and outlook of the British with the clarity—perhaps false clarity— which can sometimes appear from off the coast of Dover of what is held in common, but unnoticed, between the natives.

He was neither the first nor the last observer to insist on the extraordinary combination of solidarity and hierarchy in British society. And his basic explanation is the long established, always dominant, force of English aristocracy. 'To the great surprise of the Continental student of England', says Dibelius, 'this matter-of-fact, practical, and conservative English character appears wherever the Anglo-Saxon is met with: the differentiation between different geographical sub-types of the race is astonishingly small.' He then goes on to put stress on the early establishment of royal absolutism in England by the Norman kings. Real variations from the type appear in Britain only outside England and the Norman sphere of influence.

Thus, the Scot was affected neither by Norman centralization, nor by a civilization based upon the Anglican Church. So, under Calvinist influences, he developed a profound habit of thought, and a one-sidedly religious character, while the wildness of his nature, half-English and half-Celtic, never fully submitted to the surface polish of an Anglo-Saxon court. The Irish, even after the loss of their language, went their own way. Visionary dreamers, capable of swift, passionate excitement, prone to swift weariness and disillusionment, and richly endowed with artistic gifts, they also have their full share of the peasant inheritance of coarse materialism, and at the centre of their inner life, in the sphere of religion and national feeling, are capable of an amazing endurance, that centuries of disappointment proved powerless to break.

In England itself, Dibelius insists that there was a homogeneous national character, even across classes. 'Apart from Scotland, English national life contrasted with the rich variations of the Continent, presents a picture of drab uniformity, fatally congenial to the creation of a featureless and spineless urban population.'[8]

These sketches of national character are amusing: they may even be true. They speak to us of stubborn historical persistence and uniformity. But what of conflict and change?

Continuity normally presupposes consensus. Change typically results from conflict. We must, therefore, explore the sources of consensus and conflict. How are differences between classes, sexes, generations, and ethnic groups to be depicted, how have they been changing, and how controlled? The answers are to be found, I think, in the relation between means and ends. The means are social organizations and movements, and these we shall consider in the following chapters. The ends are the ideals which dominate modern social thought—what I have referred to as the dreams of the modern age. They are Liberty, Equality, and Fraternity. They are, so to say, courts of appeal before which policy and practice appear as plaintiffs or defendants in an evolving trial of promise and performance. As society develops, it is through various combinations of these three ideals that scholars abstractly, and ordinary people concretely, assess the quality of that development. And in this complex interplay of social action and reflections upon it, we can discern two contending traditions—the one liberal, evolutionist, and long-suffering, giving highest priority to liberty; the other socialist, revolutionary, critical, and giving highest priority to equality. What is most clearly evident from the British experience, in my opinion, is an unresolved problem of fraternity or basis for social order beneath the clash of egalitarian and libertarian argument. This argument is central to political debate. Fraternity, for all its relevance is somehow left to moralists and theologians.

Yet, as I understand it, fraternity is sociologically prior to liberty and equality. All three principles are difficult to define. All three have a subjective as well as an objective aspect: they are all, in other words, both abstractions about the experience of people in their dealings with others as well as phenomena which can be observed by our Martian visitor as behaviour. But the priority of fraternity is that it is the principle which defines the *group* within which certain social *values* are to be applied. These values are essentially those of recognizing a common humanity: quintessentially they consist for each individual in recognizing the value of life for the other and the common fate of death for all. But the totality of social morality covers many more features of social life. Social moralities may be restricted with respect to either the group within which they are applied or in the extent that others are treated as equivalent to self. The moral community is bounded by these restrictions. Primitive man, characteristically, made linguistic distinctions at the boundary of the tribe to exclude the outsider from access to the humanity attributed to the insider. Every case of racism or sexism, or class or status distinction is to some greater or lesser extent such a restriction. The subjective feeling of fraternity is that of brotherhood: the objective behaviour is that of altruism. But this brotherhood may be exclusive or universal. The mark of the world religions is that they discovered and proclaimed the species as the only group boundary. As St. Paul put it in the famous letter to the Ephesians (4: 25), 'We are members one of another'. The code of conduct enjoined by universal fraternalism is expressed most graphically in the story of the Samaritan. Sociologically, then, we mean by fraternity that, objectively, a collectivity in which the fraternal principle operates is one in which the members are integrated in their relations to one another by a set of distributional rules in which all are implicated and in which all share. Yet a fraternal society need be neither liberal nor egalitarian. Fraternity may be linked to liberty in that the liberty in question may be held to be a right for, and an obligation upon all. Fraternity may be linked to equality in that the values to be distinguished are held, in some sense, to be everyone's equal due. But liberty and equality can operate as social principles only within the bounds set by fraternity.

Equality, by contrast with fraternity, occupies an extensive place in sociological writing. There is broad agreement that society always and everywhere, though it constitutes a powerful apparatus of survival for its members, is also a structure of inequality. But sociologists differ as to the origin and development of inequality, and therefore draw different conclusions as to how it persists, and to what extent it can be modified, if not eliminated.

The sources of inequality are of two fundamental kinds. On the one hand, individuals have *interests* in life. If we assume, as we must, that there is scarcity in the means available to satisfy wants, desires, or appetites, then interests potentially imply conflict. On the other hand, human beings are, whatever else they are, *evaluating* animals: they have preferences; they distinguish between better or worse in all things, and thus continually judge themselves and others with respect to all human attributes and behave accordingly towards each other. It thus comes about that there are hierarchies of virtue, taste, sexual attractiveness, occupational skill, artistic talent, sporting prowess, and so on. Social relations reflect these as invidious comparisons, deference and disrespect, admiration and contempt. Evaluation, given scarcity, also implies conflict.

Sociological thought tends to divide according to the emphasis put on interest as distinct from evaluation, in explaining the social origins of inequality. The fact that both interests and evaluations are created and maintained by society itself is not in question. Nor is the fact of scarcity. The capacity of human beings to consume or hoard is unlimited, and the thirst for honour and power may be insatiable. As Thomas Hobbes said:

Felicity is a continuall progresse of desire, from one object to the other; the attaining of the former being still but the way to the later . . . So that in the first place, I put as the general inclination of all mankind, a perpetual and restlesse desire of Power after power, that ceaseth onely in Death . . . because he cannot assure the power and means to live well, which he hath present, without the acquisition of more . . . and when that is done, there succeedeth a new desire; in some, of Fame from new Conquest; in others, of ease and sensuall pleasure; in others of admiration, or being flattered for excellence in some art, or other ability of the mind.[9]

If this is so, then the problem would appear to be not so much how conflict arises, but how civil society exists at all.

In this division of sociological thought, Marxists start from the primacy of interests, and liberals start from the primacy of evaluations. Their accounts of social change differ accordingly. For Marx and followers, both continuity and change are systematically built into the history of all societies in the form of a class struggle. The social relations of people are fundamentally determined by their attachment to the means whereby they wrest a living from nature—that is, the productive system of their day. The ensuing principle of distribution is exploitation. The consequent view of British history in our time is of class struggles against inequality. There is no national or international fraternity, only class solidarity and such liberty as is consistent with maintaining the dominance of a capitalist class— a dominance which necessarily imposes unequal rewards and opportunities.

For liberals, by contrast, the maintainance of civil society, as well as its improvement, operates through tastes, preferences, and human values. Society changes through the inventive activity of individuals seeking to satisfy their preferences. The principle of distribution on this view is competition. The liberal version of historical experience emphasizes the expansion of liberty through the development of free economic and political activity. Expansion is the watchword, whether in markets, or education, or culture. Expansion gradually assimilates every man into the material and cultural privileges previously enjoyed by a minority. Expansion also equalizes, but by granting new opportunities, not by curtailing existing freedoms. Fraternity consists essentially in this universal offer of new opportunity.

Again, for the Marxist, social ideas and attitudes are controlled by the ruling class. Order is maintained, at least in
the short run, by monolithic control. For the liberal, on the
other hand, society is pluralistic and status groups, family,
school, church, and voluntary organizations, can play independent roles as bearers of socializing or civilizing influence.

So we inherit two fundamentally opposed theories of
history. One has set Eastern Europe on the path to Communism. The other has been tested in our own time and in
Western Europe. They are both, of course, children of the
same historic European convulsion, but our immediate concern is with Britain. For Britons, the triad of social aspirations descends in popular imagination from the slogans
carried across Europe by French revolutionary soldiers after
the fall of the *ancien régime*. But a competent Chinese his-
torian would pay scant attention to what he would see as
the trivial tribal boundaries of European states. He would
note that these political proclamations were to be heard in
Manchester as well as in Paris in the 1790s—that is to say,
in the heartland of the economic as distinçt from the political territory of a Western Europe which was modernizing
itself in the late eighteenth and early nineteenth centuries.

Professor Hobsbawn, adopting on this occasion an im-
peccably Chinese view, has graphically described all this in
his book *The Age of Revolution*. The old society of hierarchy, order, duty, and reciprocity was to be replaced by
one of democratic fellowship in a society of free men asso-
ciating together on equal terms. True that two of the three
principles—equality and freedom—could be shown in some
ways to oppose and in more ways to limit each other in the
actual social relations of people. These oppositions and
limits have absorbed the attention of social scientists down
to our own day. We still find them ranged from the aggres-
sive libertarianism of Milton Friedman,[10] through the
gentler accommodations to the egalitarianism of Isaiah
Berlin,[11] or the 'new liberty' to which Ralph Dahrendorf
devoted his Reith Lectures,[12] on through the argued
egalitarian liberalism of John Rawls,[13] to the radical egalitarianism of R. H. Tawney.[14]

What again I find puzzling and elusive in all this literature is the problem of fraternity. The Marxist analysis, in
effect, postpones it until after the postulated revolution.
But liberal doctrine does not admit this evasion. Here it is,
I think, that Professor Hirsch, in a remarkable book, has
posed the problem most sharply. Economic growth, of
which Britain was the leader in the first half of the nineteenth century, might appear to offer a way out of the
Hobbesian tragedy. And modern political promises to en-
large and spread material abundance seem to reassert that
promise. But it cannot be so. As Professor Hirsch argues,
there are social limits to growth.[15]

We can see these limits if we follow Hirsch and distinguish two economies: one in *material* goods, and the other
in *positional* goods. Material goods like tea or mugs can be
expanded in their supply practically without limit. But
positional goods are in more or less fixed supply. If we
have a monarchy, only one of us can be queen: only 49 per
cent can enjoy superior amenities. There is a range of positional goods such as old masters, suburban houses, and the
Wardenship of Nuffield College which are fixed or scarce
in some socially imposed sense or spoilt if more extensively
used. The market for them is a zero sum game—if you win
I lose—or even a negative sum game, in that people consume
resources in mutually cancelling efforts to gain market advantage. Hirsch's thesis is, then, a re-statement of the
Hobbesian problem applied to the special conditions of
modern Britain where economic liberalism, as he puts it,
is 'the victim of its own success'. He argues that affluence
presents a new form of the old problem of reconciling
limited means to unlimited ends. 'The liberal capitalist
order', he says, 'was associated with what can now be seen
as transient inaugural conditions. First, full participation
was confined to a minority—the minority that had reached
material affluence before liberal capitalism had set the
masses on the path of material growth.' But the story of
Britain in the twentieth century, as in other industrial
countries, is undoubtedly one of gradually increasing demand for full participation in the 'good life'.[16] And *pari*

passu, it becomes increasingly clear that the economic liberalism which encourages self-interest (or liberty) runs against the no less pressing need for a social morality of obligation, if markets are to be free and efficient. As Emile Durkheim argued, 'There is more to the contract than the contract.'

Here again, then, is the problem of fraternity. Its origins lie in the intrinsic character of scarcity as an essential feature of society which also gives rise to a perennial problem of inequality in the distribution of power and advantage. Scarcity will always bring us back to the problem of fraternity. In present-day discussion, the characteristic and confused expression of this problem is a familiar and widely expressed fear of the fragility of our social order. In that form it appears as the comprehensive proposition that British society faces imminent disaster. The proposition is that Britain has declined, is declining, and will shortly collapse. There are many versions of it short of apocalyptic prophecy with which no sociologist is equipped to deal. The secular versions point to the threats to institutions which are necessary to ensure our survival, banal as it may be to say so. Thus Britons must produce and the economy is held to be faltering. And Britons must reproduce, yet it is widely argued that their institutions of kinship and upbringing are in increasing disarray.

Some Conservative politicians tend to describe current British conditions in terms of the eleventh hour at which the country must turn back, or give itself up to Socialist tyranny. Some Marxists hail what they term 'contradictions' as evidence of the end of capitalist society and the approaching revolution. Even the Labour Party, the main bearer of political cheerfulness in our time, has lately tended to see North Sea oil as a last chance to modernize the British economy and society. No industrial technology is without a scientist to forecast its demise: no political party, Labour, Conservative, Liberal, or Communist, is without a political scientist to predict its break-up and the end of parliamentary institutions. Nor do anticipations of mortality stop at the economy and the state. The institutions of reproduction, that is, the family and the school, have collected to themselves a chorus of equally gloomy forecast over the past generation: and with them, according to many intellectuals, go the foundations of authority and the maintainance of cultural standards.

Here is Lord David Cecil's expression of the thesis: he is looking back in 1973 to the death of his grandfather, Lord Salisbury, in 1903.

My grandfather died that evening, as the sun was setting.

This sunset, as subsequently historians have not failed to point out, was symbolic; and not just of my grandfather's death. To the contemporary observer his career had remained to its close a success story. He died still a revered national figure, with his party in power and his policies apparently successful: he had been Prime Minister of England at the Diamond Jubilee of 1897, which celebrated the highest point of dominion and glory ever attained by the English. In fact Fate, in a spirit of irony which my grandfather would have appreciated, if grimly, had designed these triumphs as though to provide a contrasting prelude to a period of spectacular catastrophe, which entailed, incidentally, the decline of most of what my grandfather had stood for: British greatness, aristocratic government, individual liberty and international peace. Within fifty years of his death, British greatness had dwindled, aristocratic government had disappeared, individual liberty had lost its prestige and England had been involved in the two greatest wars in the history of mankind.[17]

Can all these authorities be wrong? Certainly it would be imprudent to ignore them. I want, therefore, to set out the main lines of argument in contemporary writing, and thus to arrive, if I can, at a more secure base for agreeing or disagreeing with what I take to be the dominant theme of current conventional wisdom.

The main lines of argument are concerned with the ends of liberty, equality, and fraternity, and they run between the two traditions of social thought to which I have referred, Marxism and liberalism. The fundamental question, as I understand it, is whether or to what extent these values can be realized in any society: and the approach to an answer is by examining twentieth-century experience of the basic institutions of one country, Britain. I have tried to illustrate the sociological method in this introductory chapter, emphasizing its focus on structures of social relations, its concern to explain both continuity and change, and its two opposed theories of history which are rooted in alternative liberal and Marxist views of the place of interests and evaluations as springs of human action.

The arrangement of the chapters which follow is guided by these themes. We begin, in Chapter 2, with the economy, asking first what is the outcome of work and how its fruits are distributed within the nation. Both economic growth and unequal distribution will be found as the main features of our description. With the facts of affluence and inequality before us, we can then ask how far inequality can be explained in terms of the class structure which has evolved in Britain as it developed from an agrarian to an advanced industrial nation.

We shall conclude from this analysis that not all inequality can be accounted for as a consequence of class. Accordingly, in Chapter 3, we shall turn to the history of status as distinct from class in Britain so as to refine our conception of stratification and to rest our explanation of inequality on a broader base.

Then, in Chapter 4, we can carry our class and status analysis further to include the power of organization or 'party' and in this way further strengthen our understanding of the changing distribution of power and advantage through economic, social, and political processes. Thus we shall have related the ends of liberty and equality to the means through which they have been sought in the institutions and organizations of class, status, and party.

At this point we will have completed our survey of Britain as a productive system—productive, that is, of material and psychic values—and we can turn, in the following Chapters 5 and 6, to the reproduction of the society and its culture through the family and education. These matters, from yet another point of view, confront us with the problem of explaining continuity and change over recent generations.

Finally, in Chapter 7, we shall attempt a composite picture of the changing state of British society, asking how liberty, equality, and fraternity interact as the underlying principles of the social order, how these interactions of consensus and conflict strengthen or weaken the integration of the United Kingdom, and what view we are to take of the wisespread opinion that Britain is in decline. The answers to these questions will in turn guide our views on the further questions of policies for the future. The claim and the aim throughout the argument is that sociological analysis is an aid to more sophisticated analysis. But it cannot carry us to final views beyond political or moral challenge. I have not hesitated to end, in Chapter 8, with a brief statement of my own preferences. It is for the reader to decide whether and how far my interpretations are consistent with the arguments leading to them. More important is the hope that he may thereby arrive more confidently at his own.

2 A class-ridden prosperity

'A class-ridden society'; that is the common judgement on
Britain made by social observers, whether delivered as praise
or condemnation. I heard this exact phrase from two foreign acquaintances revisiting the island this year after an
interval of ten years. Both sociologists, but the one a Russian Communist, and the other an American liberal. The
Russian spoke of the continuing hegemony of a capitalist
class with its power legally based on concentrated ownership of property and its control operating both through
the direct employment of labour and through the state apparatus of budgetary manipulation of the level of employment, definition of welfare spending, domination of the
mass media and, in the last resort, disposition of the means
of violence through the armed forces and the police. He
gave me, in short, a brief recital of Marxist orthodoxy in
which every significant feature of social structure and the
distribution of life-chances rests fundamentally on the
present sovereignty and approaching overthrow of a capitalist class.

The American used the phrase with a tone and in a context which changed its meaning. There has been economic
growth, he thought, slower perhaps but essentially similar
to that of the Continent. Nevertheless, class was still the
outstanding feature of British society: neither the élite establishment nor the attitudes of lower-class people had really
changed. That, he added, is the reason why Britain still has
the highest quality television in the world: a series like last
year's adaptation of Robert Graves's *I Claudius* would be
impossible in mainstream America; and so would the Reith

Lectures. Nowhere else in the Western world does the élite retain the confidence both to indulge its own cultural tastes and also to believe that these should be offered to or imposed didactically upon the mass of the population. The American upper class just doesn't have that status any more. He gave me, in short, a nostalgic anglophile expression of the liberalism which regrets what it sees as the inevitable sacrifice of quality when democracy is triumphant. Here then is the large theme for this second chapter. Why is it that, though Britain has become a rich country, social inequality is a continuing feature of its internal life?

In looking for an answer to this question, and noting the different words used by my American and Russian colleagues, we shall be carried to the centre of the debate about Britain among sociologists. Quite apart from the contrasting explanations of my visitors, their terminology is confusing. It includes references to upper, lower, capitalist, and working classes, to élites, the establishment, status, mass, and power. My first task, therefore, is to assemble a clear vocabulary. Fortunately this has been emerging in post-war sociological writing.

When sociologists speak of a structure of inequality they refer to the ways in which power and advantage form a stratified system of relations. By power they mean the resources which individuals or groups use to have their will, irrespective of the will of others. A board of directors can close a plant: a union can strike. By advantage, they mean control over things which are valued and scarce, such as the wealth of a millionaire, or the skill of a surgeon. Power and advantage are convertible. Together they define the character of strata and the relations between them in a stratification system. This system has three dimensions or forms of organization through which power and advantage are distributed.

The three dimensions are class, status, and party. Classes— for example, professional people or factory workers—are formed socially out of the division of labour. They make up more or less cohesive and socially conscious groups from those occupational groups and their families which share similar work and market situations. Status is formed out of the no less fundamental tendency of human beings to attach positive and negative values to human attributes, and to distribute respect or honour and contempt or derogation accordingly: status groups, for example peers of the realm or vagrants, form as social networks of those who share similar social prestige or life-style. Parties form out of the organized pursuit of social objectives; they are political parties, pressure groups, associations, and unions of those who consciously share a planned movement for the acquisition of power. In short, classes belong to the economic, status groups to the social, and parties to the political structure of society.[1]

Status and party will concern us in my third and fourth chapters. Here and now my task is to see how far inequality can be explained by class. But again, there is a welter of confusing terms. One thing is broadly agreed. Britain held a special historical place as the first industrial nation, which made it in the nineteenth century the classic home of an urbanized industrial working class or proletariat. But there agreement ends, and there is sharp debate about its older and its more recent history of a shifting balance of power and advantage.

A proletariat implies a bourgeois or capitalist class, and here it is essential to appreciate the long pre-industrial history of a landed aristocracy and gentry into which that capitalist class was absorbed. With due allowance for its sustained willingness and capacity to assimilate new elements, it may be said that an essentially hereditary medieval estate was slowly transformed into a fully developed class, retaining its hereditary character in a period stretching from late medieval times almost to our own day. There was no overt political revolution of the bourgeoisie. Control of state power and cultural advantage was virtually unbroken in the long journey from agrarian feudalism to industrial capitalism. The muddle of adjectives to denote classes comes from this history so that the terms upper, leisured, middle or middling, and lower are verbal deposits from the earlier pre-industrial age. It was the nineteenth-century analysts

of industrial society who identified classes as capitalist,
bourgeois, proletarian, and working. So the peculiarity of
the British case is the mixture of confusing terms, reflecting history rather than logic. One consequence is that, in
trying to name the classes which have evolved out of industrialism, Britons frequently divide themselves not into
an upper and a lower but, absurdly, into a middle and a
working class.

But the essential point is that in industrial society the
anatomy of class is displayed in the occupational structure.[2]
Groups and individuals differ first according to the terms
on which they can sell their skills and their labour on the
market, and second according to the actual conditions of
their work—its autonomy, or lack of it, its intrinsic satisfactions, and its attendant amenities. True, the British retain
the archaic customs of an honours system through which
they translate occupational achievement into feudal rank.
They pretend, in other words, that power and advantage
derive not from activity in the labour or capital markets,
but from birth and breeding. True, too, that part of all
social inheritance is immutable: birth gives us a family of
origin, sex, race, and nationality. Some medieval estates—
an extreme form of status—were legally hereditary. Class,
too, in its fully developed form, shares this hereditary
quality: but its foundation is in the market, not the law.
An individual may move between classes in his own lifetime.
The rise and fall of classes themselves is a broader and usually longer historical process through changes in the economy and polity which may be intended or unintended,
violent or peaceful. Whether we follow the original Marxist
orthodoxy and hold that legal ownership of the means of
production is the crucial distinction or whether, with later
writers like Dahrendorf,[3] we prefer to concentrate on authority in the organization of work, classes emerge out of
occupational structure, and power and advantage are unequally distributed between them.

It is this definition of class in terms of occupation, which
is widely used in European sociology, that I shall be using
in this book. To do so implies adherence to no rigid

orthodoxy as to the number of classes in twentieth-century Britain, or to any preconception of their historical role, past or future. The number of classes that may be identified at any point of time is partly a matter of convenience directed towards the degree of refinement required for the analysis of occupational-based power and advantage. For our purposes in this book—the analysis of Britain within living memory—it will usually suffice to distinguish three classes—the middle, lower-middle, and working classes.

The first stratum can be taken to mean what most people mean by the *middle class*: professional, managerial, and administratively occupational groups and higher technicians, and their wives and children—the 'service class'. The second stratum is a heterogeneous *lower-middle class* of non-manual empolyees, small proprietors, self-employed artisans—the petite bourgeoisie or lower-middle class—but also lower-grade technicians and supervisors of manual workers who might be thought of as a 'blue-collar élite'. The third stratum is the *working class*—industrial manual workers, and agricultural workers whether skilled, semi-skilled, or unskilled. Nevertheless, the reader should be aware that more refined class schema may be used, and indeed would be necessary, to identify groups with more homogeneous market and work situations.[4]

At the beginning of the century the occupational division of labour in Britain was such that over three-quarters of the employed and self-employed population were engaged in manual work. Of these, 28.7 per cent were skilled, 34.3 per cent semi-skilled, 9.6 per cent unskilled, and 1.8 per cent were self-employed artisans in 1911. Above these manual workers stood a white collar and professional class, more confidently divided then than now into the upper-middle class and lower-middle class. And above these stood the tiny group of a few thousand—the group which Lord David Cecil, whom I quoted earlier, termed 'the governing class' of his grandfather's day. By mid-century the proportion of manual workers had fallen below two-thirds and since then it has fallen still further to roughly a half. So the first impression is of a gradual movement away from

what might be called a proletarian society: and this transformation has been gathering pace in recent decades.

By 1971, as John Goldthorpe and Catriona Llewellyn
have described it,[5] the occupational structure was more
differentiated and more balanced. In the middle there were
now three main blocks of comparable size, each accounting
for one-fifth to one-quarter of the total. There were first
the semi-skilled manual workers, second the skilled manual
workers, and third the clerical and sales workers. Flanking
these three groups were three other small groups, each between 7 per cent and 15 per cent of the total—on the one
side the unskilled workers, and on the other the professional and technical workers and the administrative, managerial, and supervisory staff.

These twentieth century shifts of occupational structure,
from the shape of a pyramid to that of an electric light
bulb, are characteristic of advanced industrial societies in
general. They are shown for Britain in Table 2.1, which
was constructed by Goldthorpe and Llewellyn. Behind
them lies economic transformation: from small to large
scale; from manufacturing to so-called tertiary sector activity; from personal dealing to bureaucracy; from handling
things to manipulating words and numbers; and from private to public organizations.

Some sociologists interpret these trends as involving the
development of a middle mass of technical and clerical employees with a consequent decline of class antagonisms, and
with the spectre of polarized capitalist society in retreat.[6]
But before drawing such inferences about Britain, it is pru-
dent to notice what is perhaps the outstanding feature of
occupational change, namely the growth of women's employment outside the home. Male and female involvement
in the economy have run different courses over the period
we are considering. As may be seen from Table 2.1, in 1911
both sexes were divided between manual and non-manual
jobs three-quarters to one-quarter. Subsequently, the female
labour force has both grown and shifted substantially into
non-manual work, so that by the 1970s three-fifths of the
employed women were non-manual while three-fifths of

Table 2.1.[1] Distribution of economically active population by occupational category, Great Britain 1911-1971, males (M) and females (F) shown separately.

Standardised census occupational category	1911 M	1911 F	1921 M	1921 F	1931 M	1931 F	1951 M	1951 F	1961 M	1961 F	1971 M	1971 F
					percentage by column							
Self-employed and higher-grade salaried professionals	1.5[a]	1.0[a]	1.6	0.9	1.7	1.0	2.8	1.0	4.5[b]	1.1[b]	6.1	1.4
Employers and proprietors	7.7	4.3	7.7	4.7	7.6	4.4	5.7	3.2	4.8[c]	3.0[c]	5.2	2.9
Administrators and managers	3.9	2.3	4.3	2.1	4.5	1.6	6.8	2.7	7.5[c]	2.6[c]	9.9	3.3
Lower-grade salaried professionals and technicians	1.4[a]	5.8[a]	1.8	6.3	1.8	6.0	3.0	7.9	4.0[b]	9.2[b]	5.5	10.8
Inspectors, supervisors and foremen[d]	1.8	0.2	1.9	0.3	2.0	0.4	3.3	1.1	3.8	0.9	4.5	1.2
Clerical workers	5.1	3.3	5.1	9.8	5.1	10.3	6.0	20.3	6.5	25.5	6.1	28.0
Sales personnel and shop assistants[e]	5.0	6.4	4.1	7.5	5.9	8.2	4.0	9.6	3.9	10.0	3.9	9.4
Skilled manual workers (inc. self-employed artisans)	33.0	24.6	32.3	20.3	30.1	19.2	30.3	12.7	32.3	10.8	29.4	9.3
Semi-skilled manual workers[f]	29.1	47.0	24.5	40.0	23.4	41.4	24.3	33.6	22.8	30.9	21.2	27.3
Unskilled manual workers[f]	11.5	5.1	16.7	8.1	17.9	7.5	13.8	7.9	9.9	6.0	8.2	6.4
Total active population (Thousands)	12,926	5,424	13,635	5,698	14,760	6,263	15,584	6,930	15,992	7,649	15,609	8,762

[1] This table was constructed by J. H. Goldthorpe and Catriona Llewellyn

Notes:

(a) Divided according to 1921 ratios. (The 1911 census did not distinguish between self-employed and salaried professionals.)

(b) Divided on the assumption of a linear trend in the ratios from 1951–1966 (sample census).

$$\text{i.e.}\quad \frac{\times 61}{\text{Total } 61} = \frac{\times 51}{\text{Total } 51} + 2/3\frac{\times 66}{\text{Total } 66} = \frac{\times 51}{\text{Total } 51}$$

(The 1961 Census did not distinguish between Self-employed and Salaried professionals.)

(c) Numbers in Groups 3 and 4 divided according to a ratio arrived at by plotting trend lines for these groups from 1951 to 1961, i.e. $P_{61} = P_{51} + 2/3(P_{66} - P_{51})$. (The 1961 Census did not distinguish between Employers and Managers.)

(d) Of manual workers.

(e) Includes supervisory personnel and also a small number of self-employed workers.

(f) Includes self-employed workers.

Sources:

The basic source is the Occupational Tables of the Censuses of Population for England and Wales and Scotland. We have, however, drawn to a large extent on the re-working of Census data by earlier investigators although modifying their procedures somewhat, and correcting what appear to be several minor errors. In various respects, therefore, our figures differ from those of our predecessors where they might appear comparable, but not to any very significant degree.

For 1911 to 1951 we began with the work of Guy Routh, *Occupation and Pay in Great Britain, 1906–60* (Cambridge University Press, 1965), Table 1, pp. 4–5, taken together with the further information provided in Appendix A, pp. 155–7.

For 1961 we have drawn on the work of G. S. Bain, *The Growth of White Collar Unionism*, (Oxford, 1970), Table 2A. 1, p. 191; and of Bain, Robert Bacon, and John Pimlott, 'The Labour Force' in A. H. Halsey (ed.), *Trends in British Society since 1900*, (Macmillan, 1972), Tables 4.1 and 4.5, pp. 113–4.

the men were still manual workers. And even the small shift to non-manual jobs among men has mostly taken place since the Second World War. What is more important about it is that the increasing numbers of higher-level professional and managerial positions have largely gone to men, while women have filled the even faster expanding array of lower white-collar jobs.

Thus, if we attach relatively greater importance from the point of view of class formation to the pattern of male employment—and this makes sense because the class, status, party, and other group affiliations of families have been principally determined by the occupational position of husbands and fathers—then the changes have been quite undramatic. The one significant change is the expansion of the professional and managerial stratum. Ralph Dahrendorf calls this the 'service class', those who provide a bridge between the rulers and the mass of the people by acting as the agents of public and private authorities.[7] In this same view the burgeoning middle mass is largely female. We know little about its impact, if any, on the degree of class polarization in Britain.

So much for a preliminary view of stratification using a simple conception of class. Now let us look at collective prosperity. At the outset, the reader should be warned against taking official estimates of the national income or the gross national product—those modern talismans of national virility—as ultimate measures of the wealth of a nation. They are the gifts of bureaucracy rather than social science. These economists' sums tell us roughly what are the products of the *occupational* division of labour: but there is a larger *social* division of labour which includes the exchanges in families, and the services of the Samaritans, as well as the fiddles unrecorded by the Inland Revenue. There is, in short, another economy of vast dimension. It was, for example, only by the fiat of the Victorian economist Alfred Marshall, that the paid labour of charwomen is counted as part of the national product, while the work of housewives is not.[8] If we were to reckon the whole output of the social division of labour it is most likely that our sterling numbers would be more than doubled. Nevertheless, if we assume that output from the two economies are in less than completely inverse relation, the official figures can be used to indicate trends. They tell us that since 1900 the United Kingdom has at least tripled its gross national product in real terms.[9]

In any case, there is general agreement that British levels of living have risen throughout the century. Indeed if that phrase is taken quite literally, it may be noted that, compared with a hundred years ago, the average Briton lives thirty years longer, mainly because of a reduction in infantile mortality. In the childhood of the oldest readers the death of a baby in the house was a grim commonplace: now, less than two in a hundred die in infancy. A narrower and more conventional measurement of living standards, by income, yields a similar ameliorative story. The median earnings of male manual workers rose from just over £1.00 a week in 1905, to just over £60.00 a week in 1976. While it is difficult if not impossible to translate these money figures into real purchasing power by discounting for inflation, we can safely say that they also represent at least a tripling of real income. Nor can there be any doubt that the ordinary manual worker and his wife are very much less the slaves of toil than they were in Edwardian England. Their market freedoms, whether as earners or spenders, have been transformed. The risk of unemployment, despite the rising rates of recent years, is much less than it was either in the inter-war years or the Edwardian period (Figure 2.1), and employment once obtained is more protected. The hours of work have been steadily reduced (from 54 to 44 between 1900 and 1970). After the Second World War, paid holidays became common and three weeks is now the norm. The official statistics for last year record 45 million holidays by residents of Great Britain.[10] This is a far cry from the experience of many, if not most, ordiary children between the wars—the annual charabanc trip to Blackpool or Skegness.

Yet inequality persists after a long period of economic growth. From this point of view the picture of prosperity

looks very different. The assumption of growing affluence
is not beyond question. The old poverties of lack of property, low pay, poor health, inadequate education, and
bad housing still disfigure, and many would say disgrace,
the powerful engine of production which we call industrial
society. The official rate of registered unemployment is

Figure 2.1. Unemployment 1921–1976 (January of each year)

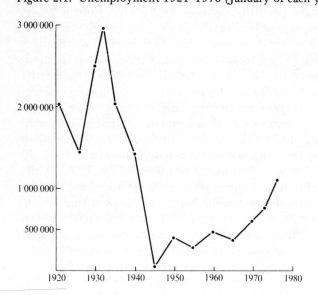

over 6 per cent of all employees. It is heavily concentrated
in the working class and within that class among the young,
the old, the sick, and the disabled. Four and three-quarter
million Britons receive money from the Supplementary
Benefits Commission. In other words, four and three-quarter million are living at the government's own estimate of
the poverty line. And there are more below it who do not
claim their due.

How, then, are income and wealth shared among the
population? Let us begin with two relatively simple statistics. In Britain now the richest 1 per cent still own one-fifth
and perhaps as much as one-quarter of all personal wealth.[11]
Income is less unequally distributed, but here again recent

official estimates show that, in 1974-5, the richest 1 per cent took home about the same amount as the poorest 20 per cent.[12] They each had, in other words, more than twenty times as much income. These are quite spectacular inequalities. We must examine their history so as to interpret them.

The trend over the past fifty years has been one of slow and unsteady progress towards a more equal distribution of personal income. By the early 1970s the top 10 per cent of income receivers were taking about one-quarter of total income, and this one-quarter share was also the amount being taken by the bottom half of income receivers. If we look at non-manual earnings a trend towards decreasing inequality is also to be seen. That trend can be traced at least as far back as the 1920s and it is still going on. Between 1968 and 1975 the ratio of non-manual to manual earnings fell from 1.24 to 1.16.

The trends in distribution of income from 1959 are shown in Table 2.2. They are taken from the most recent report of the Royal Commission on the Distribution of Income and Wealth.[13] The Commission summarizes them as follows:

Over the whole of the period from 1959 to 1974/5, the share of the top 1 per cent has declined continuously; the share of the next 2-5 per cent has declined but not continuously; the share of the 6-10 per cent group has shown little change. The share of the top 10 per cent as a whole in the before tax distribution has fallen from 29.4 per cent of total income in 1959 to 28.0 per cent in 1967 and to 26.6 per cent in 1974-5. Over the same period (1959 to 1974-5) the share of the top 1 per cent has fallen from 8.4 to 6.2 per cent of total income. The decline in the income share of the top 10 per cent as a whole is balanced by a corresponding increase in the overall share of the remaining 90 per cent, within which only one decile— 61-70 per cent—did not increase. Approximately three-fifths of this increase accrued to the remaining 40 per cent of tax units in the top half of the distribution. Their share increased from 47.5 per cent to 49.2 per cent of total income between 1959 and 1974-5 while, over the same period, the share of the bottom 50 per cent of tax units increased from 23.1 per cent to 24.2 per cent of total income.

But we have yet to consider the redistributive activity of the State. The impact of taxes and transfers is a complicated

Table 2.2. Distribution of personal income—Blue book; 1959 to 1974/5

Percentage shares of income, before income tax, received by given quantile groups; 1959, 1964, 1967 and 1968-69 to 1974-75

United Kingdom   Income unit: tax unit

Quantile group	Before income tax										Income range 1974-75 (lower limit)
	1959	1964	1967	1968-69[1]	1969-70[1]	1970-71	1971-72	1972[2][3]	1973-74	1974-75	£ pa
	%	%	%	%	%	%	%	%	%	%	
Top 1 per cent	8.4	8.2	7.4	7.1	7.0	6.6	6.5	6.4	6.5	6.2	8,585
2-5 ,, ,,	11.5	11.3	11.0	10.7	10.8	11.1	11.0	10.8	10.6	10.6	4,983
6-10 ,, ,,	9.5	9.6	9.6	9.3	9.4	9.8	9.8	9.7	9.7	9.8	4,097
Top 10 per cent	29.4	29.1	28.0	27.1	27.2	27.5	27.3	26.9	26.8	26.6	4,097
11-20 ,, ,,	15.1	15.5	15.2	15.4	15.5	15.9	15.9	15.8	15.6	15.8	3,238
21-30 ,, ,,	12.6	12.6	12.6	12.9	13.0	13.2	13.2	13.1	12.9	13.1	2,732
31-40 ,, ,,	10.7	10.9	11.1	11.0	10.9	11.0	11.0	11.0	11.2	11.0	2,296
41-50 ,, ,,	9.1	9.2	9.1	9.4	9.4	9.0	9.2	9.2	9.3	9.3	1,913
51-60 ,, ,,	7.5	7.4	7.7	7.6	7.6	7.4	7.4	7.5	7.5	7.6	1,509
61-70 ,, ,,	5.9	5.8	6.0	6.2	6.1	5.9	5.9	5.9	5.8	5.8	1,168
71-80 ,, ,,	4.4	4.3	4.8	4.7	4.7	4.6	4.5	4.8	4.7	4.6	909
81-90 ,, ,,	5.3	5.2	3.4	3.4	3.3	3.1	{ 5.6	} 5.8	3.5	3.6	680
91-100 ,, ,,			2.2	2.3	2.2	2.5	{	}	2.7	2.6	—
Differences as a percentage of the median between upper and lower quantile	98	103	91	97	99	106	105	101	102	102	—
Median £ pa	514	679	843	909	985	1,050	1,180	1,338	1,550	1,913	—
Gini coefficient %	39.8	38.9	38.2	37.4	38.0	38.5	38.3	37.4	37.0	37.1	—
Number of tax units covered (millions)	26.5	27.5	27.8	28.1	28.2	28.2	28.2	28.4	28.1	28.3	—

Source: *Royal Commission on the Distribution of Income and Wealth* Report No. 5. Cmnd 6999, Table 5, 1977.

one and much debated. It operates, as R. M. Titmuss pointed out,[14] through three loosely related systems of state intervention—fiscal policy, the social services, and occupational welfare. Essentially these political interventions can only be understood as collective action to change the unacceptable outcome of market exchanges: and that means the outcome of class. Historically, the development of these elements of social policy starts from the liberal governments before the First War. Their complexity mirrors the increasing complexity of the division of labour. They give Britain now a social division of welfare which is not by any means simply a political antidote to class distribution of what is produced by collective labour. On the contrary, social policy itself has been powerfully shaped by class. For example, the fiscal system has been no simple extension of progressive taxation from its introduction in 1907. Some details from 1959 are given in Table 2.3. By 1974/5 before tax the richest 10 per cent took 26.6 per cent of income, and this was reduced to 23.2 per cent by taxation. At the lower end, the poorest 10 per cent took 2.8 per cent before tax, and this was increased to 3.1 per cent after tax. These figures can scarcely be interpreted as evidence of a hugely distributive 'welfare' state. Welfare, it would appear, is largely self-financed for the bulk of the population. The activity of the state makes for no dramatic reduction of market inequalities.

Similarly, the social services are not to be thought of as a steady development of 'class abatement' through politics. In education, for example, throughout the twentieth century, a policy of expansion has been frequently justified as a means to equality of opportunity. But in spite of a slight tendency to more equal investment in the school education of children from different classes, the development of further education more than counter-balanced this equalizing effect because it was concentrated on middle-class children. If we compare boys born between 1913 and 1922 with those born between 1943 and 1952 (and standardize the figures by putting them into 1958 prices), it turns out that the average son of a professional or managerial family

Table 2.3. Effect of income tax on the Blue book distribution of personal income 1959 to 1974/5

Percentage shares of income before tax, average tax paid as percentage of income before tax, and percentage shares of tax paid; by quantile groups of income before tax; 1959, 1967, 1972–73, 1973–74 and 1974–75

United Kingdom

Income unit: tax unit

Quantile group of income before tax	Percentage share of income before tax					Average tax paid as percentage of income before tax					Percentage share of tax paid				
	1959	67	72-73	73-74	74-75	1959	67	72-73	73-74	74-75	1959	67	72-73	73-74	74-75
	%	%	%	%	%	%	%	%	%	%	%	%	%	%	%
Top 1 per cent	8.4	7.4	6.3	6.5	6.2	43.2	43.3	41.6	42.0	47.1	34.5	23.3	18.4	17.7	15.8
2-5 ,, ,,	11.5	11.0	10.8	10.6	10.6	19.1	20.6	22.6	21.9	25.4	20.2	16.1	16.7	15.1	14.8
6-10 ,, ,,	9.5	9.6	9.7	9.8	9.8	11.3	14.6	16.9	18.6	21.8	10.2	10.6	11.6	11.4	11.6
Top 10 per cent	29.4	28.0	26.8	26.8	26.6	23.5	24.5	25.1	25.6	29.1	64.9	50.0	46.7	44.2	42.2
11-20 ,, ,,	15.1	15.2	15.8	15.6	15.8	7.8	13.3	15.1	15.8	19.3	11.6	15.0	16.5	16.2	16.6
21-40 ,, ,,	23.3	23.7	24.2	24.1	24.1	5.7	11.1	12.9	14.5	17.2	13.1	19.5	21.8	22.7	22.8
41-60 ,, ,,	16.6	16.8	16.7	16.7	16.9	4.9	9.1	10.4	12.1	15.2	7.8	11.4	12.1	13.1	14.1
61-80 ,, ,,	10.3	10.7	10.7	10.5	10.4	2.6	4.7	3.8	5.3	7.2	2.6	3.7	2.9	3.6	4.0
81-100 ,, ,,	5.3	5.6	5.8	6.3	6.2	0.1	0.8	—	0.4	1.0	—	0.4	—	0.2	0.3
All groups	100.0	100.1	100.0	100.0	100.0	10.5	13.6	14.4	15.4	18.3	100.0	100.0	100.0	100.0	100.0

Note: — indicates less than 0.1.
Source: pre-1974–75 figures derived from Blue Book; 1974–75 figures derived from CSO table in Economic Trends, April 1977.

United Kingdom

Income unit: tax unit

Quantile group	After income tax										Income range 1974-75 (lower limit)
	1959	64	67	68-69[1]	69-70[1]	70-71	71-72	72-73	73-74	74-75	£ pa
	%	%	%	%	%	%	%	%	%	%	
Top 1 per cent	5.3	5.3	4.9	4.6	4.7	4.5	4.6	4.4	4.5	4.0	5,856
2-5 ,, ,,	10.5	10.7	9.9	9.8	9.7	10.0	10.0	9.8	9.8	9.7	3,846
6-10 ,, ,,	9.4	9.9	9.5	9.2	9.2	9.4	9.5	9.4	9.3	9.5	3,260
Top 10 per cent	25.2	25.9	24.3	23.6	23.6	23.9	24.1	23.6	23.6	23.2	3,260
11-20 ,, ,,	15.7	16.1	15.2	15.5	15.6	15.9	15.9	15.8	15.5	15.8	2,670
21-30 ,, ,,	12.9	12.9	13.0	13.1	13.3	13.3	13.4	13.2	13.2	13.2	2,250
31-40 ,, ,,	11.2	11.1	11.0	11.5	11.4	11.2	11.3	11.2	11.2	11.4	1,926
41-50 ,, ,,	9.9	8.8	9.7	9.7	9.7	9.5	9.4	9.5	9.5	9.4	1,604
51-60 ,, ,,	7.2	8.0	7.7	8.1	8.1	7.8	7.8	8.0	7.8	7.8	1,315
61-70 ,, ,,	6.6	5.6	7.1	6.6	6.7	6.5	6.4	6.5	6.4	6.4	1,080
71-80 ,, ,,	5.2	5.1	4.9	5.3	5.2	5.2	5.1	5.5	5.4	5.3	870
81-90 ,, ,,	}6.0{	}6.5{	}7.1{	6.6 {}	6.4 {}	6.7 {}	6.6 {}	6.8 {	4.2	4.4	676
91-100 ,, ,,									3.2	3.1	—
Median £ pa	477	596	758	819	870	924	1,031	1,187	1,348	1,604	—
Number of tax units covered (millions)	26.5	27.5	27.8	28.1	28.2	28.2	28.2	28.4	28.1	28.3	—

Source: 1974-75 figures derived from CSO table in Economic Trends, April 1977; 1968-69 to 1971-72 figures derived from data supplied by the CSO; figures for other years derived from Blue Book.

Note: In some years the income share of the lower quantile groups cannot be estimated with any degree of confidence as the published range tables have too few income ranges at the lower end of the distribution to permit successful interpolation.

Changes in quantile shares of the order of 0.1 percentage points are within the margin of error of the estimates.

[1] The estimates for the earliest years in the financial year series are rather uncertain because of the difficulty of analysing the available data retrospectively (see paragraph 60).

Source: Royal Commission on the Distribution of Income and Wealth. Report no. 5, Cmnd 6999. Table 4.

had seven times as much spent on him as the son of an agricultural labourer in the earlier period, and six times as much
in the later period. A comparison of these First War and
Second War children in absolute terms shows that the
average professional son got an extra £566 a year for education after school, and the agricultural labourer's son an
extra £103 a year as a result of the intervening expansion
of educational opportunity.

Again, the third system of occupational welfare is more
of a complement than a counterweight to class inequality.
Occupational pensions are earnings-related. Sick pay and
pension arrangements are better for non-manual than for
manual workers. And there has been a considerable growth
of tax-deductable fringe benefits since the war with the
effect of increasing inequality between highly paid execu-
tives and the rest.

In the argument up to this point we have documented
continuing, if slowly decreasing, income differences: and
we have shown that they are related to class. But the more
challenging task is to explain them. For orthodox Marxists
the distribution of capital is crucial: it fundamentally defines the class structure. Professor Westergaard and Miss
Resler, who have produced a voluminously and soberly
argued empirical account from the Marxist standpoint, conclude that it was the exceptional circumstances of war
which produced lasting effects on the contrasts in income
and wealth. They insist, however, that the two wars

formed no part of a continuous trend toward equalization, and that
they entailed only modest redistribution . . . Disparities may indeed
have widened since the 1950s. They certainly did not narrow significantly, from the early 1950s to the early 1970s under governments
of either political shade.[15]

Moreover, these authors find the root cause of continuing
inequality in the condition of property-less labour of most
people: and this in turn they attribute primarily to the
concentration of property ownership. 'It is for that reason
above all,' they argue, 'that capitalism can make no claim
to a steadily more equal spread of wealth. Inequality is entrenched in its institutional structure.'[16]

Liberal theorists, for their part, do not deny the inequality of distribution of personal wealth. But they do not accept the importance that Marxists attach to it, and would contest the further Marxist theory that status and power in society are derived from it. Instead, they begin by arguing the significance of trends towards a more equal spread of both wealth and income. Argument about the exact measure of the distributions themselves is relatively unimportant. The various authorities would agree that the proportion of personal wealth held by the richest 1 per cent of the population before the First World War was about 70 per cent. By the mid 1930s it was reduced to 56 per cent, and by 1960 to 42 per cent. Subsequent official figures are on a slightly different basis. They show the percentage held by the top 1 percent of people as moving down from 37 per cent in 1962, to 26 per cent in 1974. More detailed figures from 1960 are reproduced in Table 2.4 from the latest report of the Royal Commission on the Distribution of Income and Wealth. At first glance, then, these figures would appear to contradict Westergaard and Resler, and to show a strong and steady trend towards equality. But essentially Westergaard is right because the redistribution has very largely been a spread of wealth to the richest 5 per cent instead of 1 per cent, and much of it reflects arrangements for gifts *inter vivos*—gifts between the living as distinct from those bequeathed at death. In this way rich families have passed on their wealth and legally avoided tax.

The technicalities leave room for further argument about the exact degree of concentration of private wealth and its long-run trends. But if following R. H. Tawney, we distinguish between property for power, by which I mean property that carries with it control over the lives of other people, and property for use, possessions that free a man from other people's control, then we can reasonably say that, throughout the period we can collectively remember, three-quarters of the British have been virtually propertyless in that area which covers the central part of life and occupations—how men and women earn a living and how they relate themselves most fully and creatively to their

Table 2.4. Trends in the distribution of personal wealth since 1960

Percentage shares of estimated personal wealth of given quantile groups both of the population covered by the Inland Revenue estimates and of the total population aged 18 and over, with Gini coefficients; at specified dates between 1960 and 1975.

Great Britain 1960-1974
United Kingdom 1974 and 1975

(Series A and B)

Quantile group	1960	1962	1964	1966	1968	1970	1972	1973	(GB) 1974	(UK) 1974	(UK) 1975
	%	%	%	%	%	%	%	%	%	%	%
Population covered by Inland Revenue estimates (Series A)											
Top 1 per cent	28.4	27.2	25.9	23.6	24.2	20.7	22.1	21.8	18.4	18.3	17.2
Top 5 per cent	50.9	48.8	48.5	43.7	45.2	40.9	41.8	38.8	36.7	36.7	35.0
Top 10 per cent	63.1	60.7	60.5	56.0	57.1	51.9	53.9	50.9	49.0	49.1	47.3
Top 20 per cent	76.2	73.9	74.1	70.8	71.2	66.4	68.5	66.6	64.9	65.0	63.3
Bottom 80 per cent	23.8	26.1	25.9	29.2	28.8	33.6	31.5	33.4	35.1	35.0	36.7
Gini Coefficient	73	72	72	67	68	65	66	65	63	63	62
Total population aged 18 and over (Series B)[1]											
Top 1 per cent	38.2	36.0	34.4	31.8	32.7	29.0	29.9	27.6	25.3	25.2	23.2
Top 5 per cent	64.3	60.7	59.3	56.7	59.0	56.3	56.3	51.3	49.9	49.9	46.5
Top 10 per cent	76.7	74.0	73.5	71.8	73.8	70.1	71.9	67.2	66.0	66.1	62.4
Top 20 per cent	89.8	88.4	88.4	87.8	89.4	89.0	89.2	86.4	85.5	85.6	81.8
Bottom 80 per cent	10.2	11.6	11.6	12.2	10.6	11.0	10.8	13.6	14.5	14.4	18.2
Gini Coefficient	89	87	87	86	87	86	86	84	83	83	81

Source: Inland Revenue.
[1] Assuming that persons not covered by the Inland Revenue estimates have no wealth.

Source: Royal Commission on the Distribution of Income and Wealth. Report No. 5. Cmnd 6999. 1977. Table 33.

fellows. A tiny minority has monopolized wealth, and an even tinier minority of that minority has monopolized property for power.

At the same time, of course, harking back to the fact of rising affluence, we should not ignore the social significance of the spread of property for use. Most of the under-40s take a wide range of amenities and consumer durables for granted. Only the over-40s remember those primitive instruments of washing day—the poss-stick and the dolly-tub.

To sum up a formidable ledger of evidence, we can say that distributions through the capital and labour markets were dramatically unequal at the opening of the century. Wealth, part of which is property for power, was always more unequally spread than income. And both distributions have remained unequal around a rising average level. Over and above such wealth for use as housing and personal possessions, property for power still has a most impressively unequal distribution. But the trend to a relatively more equal sharing of income has increasingly dominated the structure of inequality as a whole because the labour market distributes much more income than does the capital market. In 1976 income from employment accounted for well over two-thirds of all income. The self-employed accounted for less than one-tenth, and so did unearned income from rent, dividends, and interest payments. On the evidence so far, then, the problem is to decide whether to attach more importance to the remaining inequality, or to the expanded material freedom which has attended the rising norm. The judgement will turn on whether one is impressed by absolute or by relative riches.

In either case, we have still not fully explained the inequality of a rich society. The question of how it has survived can again be put in class terms by quoting what J. B. Priestly had to say on his journey through England in 1933, when he came to Jarrow—a wholly working-class town.

Wherever we went there were men hanging about, not scores of them but hundreds and thousands of them. The whole town looked as if it had entered a perpetual penniless bleak Sabbath. The men wore the masks of prisoners of war. A stranger from a distant civilization, observing the condition of the place and its people, would have arrived at once at the conclusion that Jarrow had deeply offended some celestial emperor of the island and was now being punished. He would never believe us if we told him that in theory this town was as good as any other and that its inhabitants were not criminals, but citizens with votes.[17]

Jarrow provides one example of the remarkable absence of resentment against class inequality. In an attempt to explain this feature of British society, W. G. Runciman has put forward the theory of relative deprivation.[18] On this theory, satisfaction or resentment is not a function of inequality as documented by economists, but of a man's assessment of his position relative to other people with whom he compares himself. In Runciman's view the period from the end of the First World War up to 1962, against a background of trends towards the equalization of class, status, and power in Britain, working-class status resentment increased, and class resentment fluctuated, but at a remarkably low level. Working men compared their lot with other people in the working class and not with non-manual groups, who, incidentally, were just as likely to feel deprived despite their objective advantages. In the decades before 1962 there was seldom a close correlation between class inequality and resentment of it. Both World Wars raised expectations and lifted the horizons of working-class people. But the egalitarian hopes thus engendered receded in both post-war periods. The economic depression of the 1930s inhibited comparisons between manual wages and white-collar salaries. After the Second World War there was widespread belief that a programme of class redistribution was taking place when in fact it was not. Runciman's 1962 survey showed that resentment was still low among working men and their wives because they compared themselves, in the traditional way, with those near to them in the factory and the neighbourhood. They did not compare themselves with barristers, or the residents of Mayfair. Relative deprivation was in fact more likely to be felt by middle-class than by working-class people.

Repeating the survey thirteen years later in 1975, W. W. Daniel found that the same patterns of restricted social horizons of comparison were still present.[19] Several years of serious inflation and still more years of high publicity to pay claims and incomes policy, had not significantly altered them. Most importantly, the more recent survey showed that people cared not so much about how other people were getting on as about how they saw their own financial position this year compared with last year. It seems that government policy for 'gentling the masses' is more likely to be successful if it looks to economic growth for all, rather than to redistribution between unequally placed groups.

The evidence of stability in the face of relative deprivation is remarkable. It would seem to run counter to the increasing frequency of hard bargaining in the 1970s, and the general tendencies for unionized workers to maximize their market power. What has been happening recently is that the representatives of groups of workers have been more ready to use wider comparative reference groups in pressing their claims than those which are common among the workers they represent.

So far, then, we have explained the continuing inequality of a rich society mainly in terms of the slow growth of prosperity and the limited social horizons of the relatively poor. This explanation, however, still leaves open the question of whether we can properly call the inequalities we have found class inequalities. If we follow post-Marxist and liberal theorists and define class in terms of occupational structure rather than capital ownership and if, further, we treat the family rather than the individual as the unit of the class system, we shall have to recognize that many inequalities are of status rather than of class—those between men and women, or between older and younger people, or between ethnic groups. For example, if we take the average earnings of all white males to be 100, the comparable figure for coloured men is 88. Nor is this inequality of earnings between ethnic groups to be explained in class terms. Within classes the differentials are still to be found except among the lower paid groups of semi-skilled and unskilled workers and personal service workers.[20]

Class, we may conclude, remains fundamental to stratification in Britain but it does not tell us the whole story.

3 The reconstitution of status

THE nineteenth century, it is sometimes said, ended in 1914, and the guns of that August opened a new era of British society. According to George Dangerfield, *The Strange Death of Liberal England*[1] occurred just before the First World War, during Asquith's Liberal government. For Lord David Cecil the sun set on the old order with the death of his prime ministerial grandfather, Lord Salisbury, in 1903. A search for exact chronological origins could occupy us endlessly in innocent debate. What matters, and what is agreed now from widely different ideological standpoints, is that the history of the twentieth century is the history of the decay of the values and status system of Victorian Britain.

This large sociological generalization is essential for understanding the daily social exchanges of a country in which the tiniest detail of manner and style was once a symbol sufficient to place a person immediately in a national and unitary hierarchy of prestige. The generalization is important also for understanding the social source of the 'declining Britain' thesis which recurs so frequently in *The Times,* and appears for that matter in the *New Statesman* when Paul Johnson writes for it. Its deeper significance, however, is in the light it throws on the persistence of class inequality. I want in this chapter to relate status to class.

These two concepts refer to the sources of consensus and conflict. Liberal nineteenth-century capitalism distributed the goods and services of an industrialized earth through the social mechanisms of the market. Distributions were therefore the outcome of interests. They arose from a division of labour which treated labour as a commodity and removed responsibility from the rich and powerful for the lives of the poor and dependent. The enlightened spokesmen of English liberal capitalism, Adam Smith, Ricardo, Bentham, and James Mill and John Stuart Mill elaborated impressive theories of personal freedom and material plenty, which, for a brief period, formed a consensus of sound opinion among all classes. But the actual outcomes of the market were impossible to justify. The dogma of *laissez-faire* was no defence against the evidence of the horrors of women's work underground, the exploitation of child labour in the mills, and the squalor of the new industrial cities. To the men and women caught up in, exhausted, and demoralized by this system, the 'free market' seemed to be a canting phrase for organized plunder. Class polarization and class antagonism emerged from the very conditions of free and equal access that established the market system in the first place. Order and control, short of brute force, which is itself incompatible with free markets, must come from consensual evaluations. A class system, therefore, can only remain free if the status system is congruent with it or subordinate to it. If, as sociologists now agree, such a supportive status system has been dissolving in Britain, then class must also have been losing its legitimacy; and its persistent inequalities are less and less protected from challenge.

This is in fact what has been happening, especially since the Second World War (which, incidentally, was itself a period of accelerated decay of traditional status assumptions).[2] In the later 1960s and in the 1970s most Britons have had the sense that the social contract is being renegotiated; that all the methods which distribute and redistribute burdens and benefits—the collective bargain, the statute, the judge's ruling, the executive decision, the routine of administration in central and local government, the customary expectations of work places and bus queues, and even the give-and-take of family life—that is the arrangements for the social division of duty, wealth, and welfare are in debate, their principles and procedures in question.

To understand these present and future issues we must return to the past and to the theory of class and status. My description of present disarray already implies that I will argue an important role for status, and later party, in understanding inequality—its continuities and its changes, and its relations to liberty and fraternity. There are two main arguments for the significance I accord to status. One is that some socially recognized distinctions which are highly salient to issues of equality, are nevertheless not a basis for class formation. Thus, once it is accepted that the family, and not the individual, is the unit of class systems, it follows that neither age-groups nor sexes can constitute classes. Yet equally clearly there are social conflicts which turn on the claims to equality of women and young people. Both groups have status disadvantages and advantages; but their *class* interests in the allocation of resources are predominantly dependent on their families, first of origin, and later of affinity.

The second main argument is that a new form of status has been advanced in the twentieth century to claim a second distribution or redistribution of goods and services through the state and based on criteria of need as distinct from purchasing power. This has been explicitly aimed against the class distributions of capital ownership, labour market earnings, and work conditions, and against the traditional status inequalities of generation, sex, and race. We shall see, in other words, that a reconstitution of status has accompanied the dissolution of the old order.

But neither of these arguments is intended to deny the stubborn capacity of class to survive, nor, still less, to argue inequality out of our way. Class systems and their inequalities are intrinsically prone to persist. They resist change in two ways. Those who do well out of them do not usually volunteer to surrender their advantages, and they also use their powers to pass on superior opportunities to their own children. And the more this happens, the more are classes formed. A fully developed class system is both a structure of market inequality and also an hereditary system of recruitment, in practice if not in theory.

All this is obvious. What is not so clear is how class and status can either support or oppose each other. Here the first thing to notice is that class power can be translated into status power and *vice versa*. Either can encroach upon the other: but the outstanding feature of social development in Victorian Britain was the usurpation of status by class. In the mid-Victorian period 'the upper class' meant gentlemen and gentlewomen, and was still basically a hereditary caste of titled persons and their families. However, this landed aristocracy and gentry had always absorbed new men, and in the last century the new rich of trade and industry were gradually drawn into it until in the end they overwhelmed it. A new upper class was welded together. By 1900 the House of Commons, previously an assembly of gentlemen, contained 250 bankers, merchants, tradesmen, stockbrokers, company directors, and the like, alongside and overlapping with 70 Lords, Baronets, and Honourables.[3]

The rise to high status of many British families in the nineteenth and early twentieth centuries, initially through class mobility, is both a myth and a reality. The stereotype is the factory owner accumulating capital in a Northern or Welsh industrial town in the first generation; the firm expands in the second generation; and in the third is a large public corporation, vertically integrated and with metropolitan headquarters. The status translation of family members runs from the original artisan—provincial, respectable, chapel-attending; the sons are educated in local grammar schools and perhaps Armstrong College in Newcastle, or Josiah Mason in Birmingham, and the grandsons in a major public school and an Oxford college. The family journey also runs from chapel to church, from Liberal to Conservative voting, from business to the major professions and management, and from the Commons to the Lords. The Herald's Office attends to the details.

This caricature indicates that, though classless societies have existed, and more are conceivable without classes, status depends in the long run on access to material resources, and such access in this case was primarily afforded through the capital and labour markets.

Edwardian Britain had a secure alliance of class with status. The bourgeoisie had adopted modified versions of the tastes and style of life of the aristocracy and the gentry. The old barriers between Church and Dissent had been widely breached, and trade had married title as Sybil had wedded Egremont in Disraeli's novel. This formidable combination dominated the manners and consciousness not only of its cadets in what Orwell called the 'lower-upper-middle class' of home and imperial administration, and not only of the slowly growing but still inferior ranks of the professions and the salariat, but also of its remote dependants beyond the great divide—the men, and particulaly the women, of the manual working class.

I say remote, and the sense in which the word remote describes the relations of the upper to the lower classes is plain enough. But for some if already a declining number of working-class families, relations were intimate through generations of domestic service. Thus, while it was true of the status order that 'an Englishman had only to open his mouth to make another Englishman despise him', the language of U and non-U was not a simple binary division barring the middle from the upper classes, but also a language linking the 'governing class' to their 'lower class' servants along a different dimension of symbolic subordination. This direct association was already declining, but its function of binding unequals together was still of some importance then. Along with the vocabulary and the routines of domestic management, larger conceptions of hierarchy and place were deferentially absorbed. An integrated inequality was the central principle of social life in Britain before the First World War.

Status control over time and social distance is one of the themes running through Robert Roberts's account of the working-class district of Salford in which he grew up in the first quarter of this century.[4] 'By 1900', he tell us, 'those cherished principles about class, order, work, thrift, and self-help, epitomized by Samuel Smiles and long taught and practised by the Victorian bourgeoisie, had moulded the minds of even the humblest.'[5]

The boys of Roberts' community avidly read *The Magnet* and *The Gem*—comic papers exalting the life and manners of public schoolboys. While they went daily to a seedy elementary school, they vicariously adopted Greyfriars as their Alma Mater. 'The "mouldering pile", one came to believe, had real existence: of that boys assured one another.' They placed it vaguely in the southern countries—somewhere between Winchester and Harrow. It came as a 'curious shock' to Roberts, who revered 'the Old School', when it dawned upon him that he himself was a typical example of the 'low cads' so despised by all at Greyfriars. 'Over the years', he claims, 'these simple tales conditioned the thought of a whole generation of boys. The public school ethos, distorted into myth and sold among us weekly in penny numbers, for good or ill, set ideals and standards.' In Roberts' opinion, 'Frank Richards during the first quarter of the twentieth century had more influence on the mind and outlook of young working-class England than any other single person, not excluding Baden Powell.'[6] Nor did these ideologies disappear with the new generation after the war. In the 1930s and '40s too, working-class boys identified no less enthusiastically with the public school heroes of 'Red Circle', the mythical public school of the *Hotspur,* and with the imperial ethic in its purest form—'The Wolf of Kabul'. The adult, and more subtle version of Harry Wharton, I might add, is Jeeves, created by P. G. Wodehouse, and widely enjoyed by a mass readership. Jeeves is essentially the servant, clearly more able than his feckless master, who nonetheless devotes a lifetime of service to the preservation of traditional privilege.

The Salford proletariat was arranged in an elaborate status hierarchy, rooted, of course, in the different market and work situations of workers with different levels of skill, but extending to cover all men, women, and children in a closed urban village of crowded streets, sharing a common culture of bare subsistence and survival. The arbiters of status in the community were women, centred on 'a powerful inner ring of grandmothers. . . .'. The poverty stricken analogue of landed possessions was not even so much what one owned by way of domestic equipment, but what one pawned. To hock clean clothes gave higher status than dirty hearth rugs, or the pots off the table. When neighbours quarrelled the symbols of status were hurled back and forth

to prove to the world that the other party and its kindred were 'low class' or no class at all. One waved, for instance, a 'clean' rent book (that great status symbol of the times) in the air, knowing the indicted had fallen in arrears. Now manners and morals were arraigned before a massed public tribunal . . . Purse lipped and censorious, the matriarchs surveyed the scene, soaking it all in, shocked by the vulgarity of it all, unless, of course, their own family was engaged. Then later, heads together, and from evidence submitted, they made grim readjustments on the social ladder.'[7]

Nor were the growth and grip of these virtues left to chance or the comic book. They were incorporated into the public agencies of child rearing throughout the nation. With a confidence now unimaginable, the Elementary School Code of 1904 delineated in exact terms the morality to be inculcated by school teachers. They were to 'implant' in the children 'habits of industry, self control, and courageous perseverance in the face of difficulties'. The Catechism of the Anglican Prayer Book, repeated millions of times by the ancestors of these urban proletarians, was not wholly forgotten in the new unnatural world of the factory town.

My duty towards my Neighbour, is to love him as myself, and to do to all men, as I would they should do unto me: To love, honour, and succour my father and mother: To honour and obey the King, and all that are put in authority under him: To submit myself to all my governors, teachers, spiritual pastors and masters: To order myself lowly and reverently to all my betters: To hurt no body by word nor deed: To be true and just in all my dealing: To bear no malice nor hatred in my heart: To keep my hands from picking and stealing, and my tongue from evil-speaking, lying, and slandering: To keep my body in temperance, soberness, and chastity: Not to covet nor desire other men's goods; but to learn and labour truly to get mine own living, and to do my duty in that state of life, unto which it shall please God to call me.

The reinforcement of class inequality by status continues to this day, but it has lost much of its Victorian and Edwardian efficacy. One cause is to be found in the transformation of the class structure itself. Although, as we have seen, inequalities persist between classes, the internal composition and hence the status assumptions and outlook of the classes have drastically changed. At one end, the old upper class of the landed aristocracy has virtually disappeared, to be replaced by a more varied collection of employers, trade unionists, politicians, administrators, and professional people, between whom social connections have loosened, to whom recruitment from white-collar and manual origins has greatly increased, and among whom there is less agreement and confidence as to the symbols of social superiority.

I have used Robert Roberts' description of Salford to illustrate the internal status structure of the urban working class in the earlier decades of the twentieth century. But in so doing, I have avoided his title, *The Classic Slum,* and this is deliberate. While it is true that Engels (in his *Condition of the English Working Class in 1844*) had used this phrase to describe the Salford through which he passed daily in the early nineteenth century, it is dangerously misleading to suggest that there was an identity between working-class communities and slums in the early part of the twentieth century. The slum existed in the Edwardian industrial town, but was typically a sharply segregated and distinctive quarter within a working-class district, within which domestic violence, child neglect, drunkenness, and the low brothel were concentrated. These quarters were in no way representative of working-class life, and the working class is wrongly and romantically depicted if it is thought of as having been rescued from the slum. Working-class districts, including those where incomes were very low, and housing and amenities poorly provided, were also areas of domestic peace and neighbourly trust of a standard which we do not know today. People never thought of locking their houses if they went out during the day, and theft would have been cause for amazement. The traditional problems of the slum have since been more widely spread through the town and cities, with the result that old working-class areas have lost their capacity to police the activities of strangers with the almost total efficiency of the period before the First World War. These districts and neighbourhoods have also lost their capacity, even if there were still the cultural aim, of 'keeping up standards', such as they were, of 'workman', 'workmate', 'neighbour', 'mother', 'housewife', etc. These standards were neither noble nor 'cultured', and indeed may be argued to have been pathetically misguided expressions of status conformity. Nevertheless, what Roberts calls 'the cherished principles' were not the values of the 'classic slum'.

Journalism and quasi social science continues to find the myth that identifies 'the working class' with the slum fatally attractive. But historical accuracy gives us a quite different picture. The point may be illustrated by recalling how Beatrice Webb made her 'romantic' discovery that there was a wage-earning family among her kith and kin whom she visited in Bacup, whence she wrote to her father in 1883:

> You would have laughed, father, to see me sitting amongst four or five mill-hands . . . I was surprised at their fair-mindedness, and at the kindliness of their view of men and things . . . This class of respectable working man . . . The old man and his daughter with whom we are staying, are a veritable study of Puritan life on its more kindly side . . .
>
> I can't help thinking that it would be well if politicians would live among the various classes they legislate for, and find out what are their wishes and ideas . . . Of course, it would be absurd to generalize from such a narrow basis: but . . . Mere philanthropists are apt to overlook the existence of an independent working class, and when they talk sentimentally of the 'people' they really mean the 'ne'er-do-wells'.[8]

This less dramatic description of the working class was no less (and probably more) typical of the first half of the twentieth century than of the 1880s when Mrs. Webb was writing. Richard Hoggart's description in *The Uses of Literacy*[9] of Hunslet in the 1920s and the '30s is a similarly accurate account of working-class life in this period.

Over the past generation, since the Second World War, and of perhaps greater import, there has developed a more homogeneous and indeed more hereditary working class in Britain. This is not, by any means, the expanded and impoverished or 'immiserated' proletariat of classical Marxist prediction. Quite the opposite. It is contracted, better off, and more collectively powerful. But it is largely recruited from second and third generation people of working-class antecedents. This development is not yet widely appreciated even by sociologists, but has emerged clearly from the recent studies of the English and Welsh population in 1972 which have been carried out at Oxford,[10] and from a parallel enquiry in Scotland. An older study led by David Glass at the London School of Economics, looking back from 1949, depicted relatively caste-like conditions at the top of British society.[11] In the post-war period, however, it is the working class which has to be thought of as closed and stable in its membership, and the middle classes as relatively open to a wider range of new recruits from different class origins. Two out of every three middle-class men today were not born into a middle-class family.

In consequence, the status claims of those with class advantages have become less clear and less confidently uttered. Appeals to blood or family connections are now seldom heard, and in any case are discordant with the meritocratic values which offer them ideological challenge in a modern industrial society. Ascription is not in practice, however, debarred from presenting itself as achievement in a competitive labour market. The older upper and upper-middle classes recruited on both criteria, but the resulting fusion of a class weakened its status pretensions: and meritocracy by definition continually invites further recruitment from below.

The development of a more homogeneous working class, with reduced differentials and therefore less sharp status distinctions between skilled, semi-skilled, and unskilled workers, had complementary effects. The skilled man's rate of wages was twice that of the labourer in 1867. By 1914 the skilled rate was about 50 per cent more than the unskilled, and by 1952 the difference had narrowed to 16 per cent.[12] The material basis for status differences within the working class was, thus, eroded.

In part, of course, the unheavenly host of ennobled or honoured leaders of the British proletariat served to maintain a modified form of the older status hierarchy. There was, it is true, debate within the socially conscious elements of the Labour movement as to whether Ramsay MacDonald should wear ceremonial dress (in fact he loved it), or Walter Citrine accept a knighthood. When, earlier, Ben Tillett was criticized for dining too often at the Ritz, he had to defend himself with the rejoinder that 'only the best is good enough for the working class'. But few advocated direct rejection of upper- and middle-class styles of life. It was a Rugby, Balliol, Church of England, middle-class socialist, R. H. Tawney, who refused a peerage in a letter to MacDonald saying that 'no cat ties a tin can to its own tail'. Nevertheless, in the process, the symbols lost some of their lustre.

In any case, the slowly growing affluence and mobility of the working class supplied the material base for new and less dependent status positions. Between the Wars these came in fantasy form from Hollywood through the screens of the local picture palaces. After the Second World War interationalized 'pop stars' were carried into every house and flat by what we now call the media. A history of football heroes would sharply illustrate the point: it would run from Eddie Hapgood of Arsenal and England in the 1930s, with short back and sides, deferential to the manager, Mr. Chapman, proud to play for his country, paid the wages of a skilled manual worker, and leaving Wembley or Highbury to return home by bus and train. By the 1970s the archetypal hero had become George Best of Manchester United, idolized by teenagers, forever flouting the authority of referees and trainers, frequenting boutiques and nightclubs, practising widely publicized sexual promiscuity, driving a Jaguar, and catching planes to Los Angeles.

Geographical mobility, quickened by the two wars, broke the grip of the working-class matriarchs. The patterns of social mobility over the past generation have had still more far-reaching effects. Men and women, moving and marrying between different occupational levels, both over the generations and also within their own working lives or careers, have become an increasingly common feature of British social life in the past half century.

The patterns are complicated. They have occurred over both long and short occupational distances; they have often involved geographical migration; they are different for men and women. Pathways through education have broadened. The net result has been an upward movement through the generations. Mobility in the course of working life has not, as some Marxists have argued, developed a counter-balancing narrowness.[13]

All this might appear, incidentally, to overturn the picture of persistent inequality that I previously drew. But this is not so. It is perfectly possible that a high degree of inequality of relative chances of mobility for people of different social origins should exist alongside high and rising absolute rates of movement between classes. Where there is an inverse correlation between class and fertility, as well as an expansion of professional and managerial jobs, this coincidence of unequal relative chances and high absolute chances of upward mobility can easily result.

I will return to a more detailed consideration of class mobility in Chapter 6. The point here is that people carry images of social worth from their older to their newer class positions, and this weakens any pre-existing accord on a hierarchy of life-styles. This is what has happened in Britain. It has added to the problems of social control, whether by employers, managers, policemen, tax gatherers, parents, or teachers. It goes, in other words, beyond class to the social order as a totality. The stabilizing force of the status order we inherited from the nineteenth century has been comprehensively dismantled. Moreover, and what is perhaps more important, attitudes of resentment to the remaining status distinctions have moved in the opposite direction; they have been strengthened. This is argued cogently by Runciman in his study of attitudes to social inequality in twentieth-century England. As he puts it, 'the magnitude and frequency of relative deprivation of status in the manual stratum has, on the whole, risen as inequality of status has declined'.[14]

Social status, then, has a peculiar history. Yet we have still to explore its most significant feature, namely the rise of citizenship as a special form of status. At this point we reach a crucial step in the discussion of class and status. What I am essentially arguing is that the Marxist emphasis on class interest trivializes status by relegating it to a subsidiary role as a more or less complicated apparatus of control over subordinate classes. At the same time, I am also arguing that the liberal emphasis on status, which comes in one form or another of a pluralistic theory of stratification, constitutes the reciprocal error—it trivializes class by denying its role in undermining the freedoms promised by a liberal society.[15] The further implication is that both theories lead to false doctrines of historical progress, and neither deals adequately with the problem of social order.

There is, however, an open channel between this Scylla and Charybdis of sociological mis-explanation. It was charted by T. H. Marshall as long ago as the 1940s.[16] Marshall avoids both traps, and accurately pictures the history of conflict in Britain over the distribution of work and reward, by postulating a developing battle between the two great *dramatis personae* of our social history—*class* operating through the labour and capital markets, and *status* operating through the political and legal systems to define the rights of citizens.

The double thrust of Marshall's theory goes to the heart of social change in twentieth-century Britain, and places contemporary struggles in the wider context of the slow development of citizenship through civil rights during the period from the middle of the seventeenth century and the revolution of 1688 to the First Reform Act of 1832—including Habeas Corpus in 1679, the abolition of press censorship, and Catholic emancipation. Quoting G. M. Trevelyan,[17] Marshall points out that by the early nineteenth century 'civil rights had come to man's estate and bore (except for the right to strike) in most essentials, the appearance they have today'. The Hanoverian epoch had established the rule of law, 'and that law, with all its grave faults, was at least a law of freedom'.[18]

Subsequently, in the nineteenth century, citizenship began slowly to acquire the dimension of political enfranchisement. Class and traditional status began a long retreat from direct control over organized politics. This conquest of politics by the principle of citizenship remained incomplete down to our own period: the enfranchisement of women was not completed until the 1918 and 1928 reforms, and the dual voting for businessmen and university graduates was not ended finally until 1948. Indeed, it can be argued that political rights were not entirely freed from their attachment as privileges to a restricted economic class to become attributes of citizenship until full manhood suffrage was adopted in 1918. In the early years of the century the registered electorate was only 60 per cent of all British men, and those left out were mostly working-class.

The development of the *social,* as distinct from the civil and political, rights of citizenship belongs preeminently to the twentieth century. The 1834 Poor Law had been the last monument to the sharp separation of social rights from the status of citizenship. The break-up of the Poor Law is the central element in the even now unfinished story of the struggle of this new status against class in our life time. Its first milestone is to be found in the legislation of the Liberal landslide government of 1906. No wonder that Robert Roberts, from the vantage point of a corner shop in a working-class street, tells us how the new old age pensioners—new, that is, since 1909—when spending their allowances of 7s. 6d. per week for a married couple,'would bless the name of Lloyd George as if he were a saint from heaven'.

Citizenship won further victories in the field of social rights as the century advanced, especially after the Second World War with the establishment of Beveridge's social security programme based on insurance, and the national health service based on direct taxation. By 1977 the 'social wage' distributed by the Welfare State had become a sizeable sum: it was nearly £1,500 a year for each member of the working population of the United Kingdom.[19] But the story remains unfinished because the two principles of distribution—class and citizenship—remain in contention. A class society uses the market as its distributive instrument. It had evolved historically under powerful impulses toward economic freedom, as Marx, as well as the liberal theorists, well appreciated. Citizenship, on the other hand, is a special form of status which looks to the state and seeks a different type of distribution which turns on the political process and on the secondary form of industrial citizenship which has developed in its wake. Citizenship is also different from class in that it is intrinsically levelling. But it is not simply an assertion of equality against freedom. As Marshall was at pains to point out, it permits sanctioned inequality, for example in advanced education, or specialized medical need.

Citizenship, we should note in this context, has been defined nationally. This point is fundamental. It has been fateful for Britain in this century that the nation state was seen as the political unit appropriate to its purpose. The emerging political organization of the working classes aimed, from the start, to conquer national politics. In so doing, it necessarily took on the immense challenge of forming a national community: for citizenship status depends for its support on fraternity. Looking at the Labour Party in this way—as a movement aspiring to transform a hierarchical social order into a national community—its handicaps become plain.

The Labour movement at the beginning of the century was based on the solidarity of local class communities. Labour markets and kinship networks were bounded by walking distances. For the vast majority of ordinary people national concerns were remote from daily life. Only war made Britons out of people whose social horizons were normally enclosed by the street, the village, or the neighbourhood. The bid for men's minds, which was made by appeals for a broader national or even international class solidarity before the First World War, was in any case weak. In peace, class solidarity was dissipated in day-to-day preoccupations with survival in the close social networks of the industrial town and the agricultural village. In war, it

retreated before the siege—solidarity of response to external threat. Both phenomena, of course, parochialism and
nationalism, may be interpreted as expressions of social
control by the governing class. But this, too, further emphasizes the barrier to national community which stood
in the way of the Labour movement. A political organization committed to universal and democratic freedom had
also to face the dilemma of either persuading the powerful
minority to join a new national community by giving up
its privileges, or forcing them to do so by reducing the economic freedoms they had previously won for themselves in
the establishing of free capitalism. Moreover, the very process of economic growth, on which state welfare depended
for its development, also involved changes in the occupational structure which steadily diminished the size of the
working class and enlarged the lower-middle and middle-class
groups of white-collar, technical, and professional people.

Class and status have, then, been in complex contention
in our time, and that contention has largely determined
the application of the social principles of liberty, equality,
and fraternity.

Perhaps the most difficult test of the strength of the
citizenship principle has been its application to the immigrant population of ethnic groups with origins in the so-
called 'New Commonwealth'—mainly from Africa, the West
Indies, India, Bangladesh, and Pakistan. These are the Black
and Brown British, small ethnic minorities in a dominantly
white society. The most recent estimate of their numbers,
including those born in Britain, was 1,771,000, forming
3.3 per cent of the total population of Great Britain in
1975-6.[20] Their contribution to births in 1975 was 6.7 per
cent.[21] Nevertheless, taking into account the age structure
of these minority groups and assuming that current law and
policy do not change, their total numbers in Great Britain
can 'be expected to increase more slowly in the future
than the average rate of about 5 per cent per annum over
the five years 1971-6. The increase over the decade to the
mid-1980s could, however, still be about one half, including
a doubling of the small numbers of people aged over 50'.[22]

The coloured ethnic groups in Britain therefore constitute a small, but significant, minority. They suffer both
class and status disadvantages and discriminations. Their
citizenship is assured in law, but fragile in practice. Their
history in Britain is a short one, dating from 1948 when
the former German pleasure cruiser, the *Empire Windrush*,
brought 492 West Indians to work in Britain. Policy towards them was timidly pragmatic. There was a restricted
pre-occupation with the facts of immigration. Thus, in the
1950s, the 'stranger hypothesis' in sociological theory[23]
was the academic equivalent of a policy of assimilation.
Academic theory and official policy were mirrors of each
other. The problem was seen as that of a small number of
newcomers who would be either willing and able to learn
a learnable British culture, or would accommodate temporarily and return whence they came. The process of assimilation assumed capacities on both sides—on the part of the
host 'to be kind to the foreigner, the poor chap can't help
it', and on the part of the immigrant to understand the
reluctance of his host to expose himself hastily or to com-
mit himself unduly by identification with a stranger whose
behaviour, by definition, was imperfectly controlled by
the tacit understandings of a complex, historically evolved,
and slowly-learned code of morals and manners. The conceived scale of the problem is well illustrated by the story
of Leary Constantine's arrival between the Wars to settle in
a mining town as a professional in Lancashire league cricket.
On the Sunday morning after his arrival he went for a walk
and, true to his nature, joined in with a group of boys
kicking a football in a side street. The first boy's greeting
was, 'Hasta been downt' pit, then?'.

But both theorists and policy makers were forced in the
1960s to recognize that the assimilationist policy was no
longer possible in the face of the rapidly increased rate of
immigration, especially from India and Pakistan, at the end
of the 1950s. Hence the 1962 Commonwealth Immigration
Act. The paradoxical consequences were a temporary reversal of the intentions of the Act which brought a sharply
increased flow of Indian and Pakistani families to settle

permanently in place of the groups of male temporary workers intending to return.

These developments undermined the assumption of the older assimilative policy that the coloured population was a homogeneous collection of individuals. This was never a fact. Distinctions have to be drawn not only between different nationalities and ethnic groups, but also within these between castes, classes, and occupations, and between individuals, families, and types of community group. E. J. B. Rose showed at the end of the 1960s that the pattern of group formations among the British coloureds was changing rapidly and in different directions among West Indians, Pakistanis, and Cypriots, as well as between the first and second generation of immigrants.[24] In particular, an unassimilated group of depressed status within the working class was being formed. More generally, the developing size and heterogeneity of the coloured population demanded not assimilation but integration where the process had to be seen as a highly differentiated one of absorption, incorporation, and accommodation to the multiple relationships of locality, occupation, politics, religion, and indeed the whole network of society.

Similarly, effective race relations policies had to take account of the facts of change in the host society. The terms of assimilation have been transformed. British society is no longer as assimilative as it was when the earlier wave of Jewish immigrants arrived at the end of the nineteenth century. There has been an 'Americanization' of British society with decreasingly certain use of informal sanctions through tacit understandings, and with growing impersonality, mobility, and aspirations towards privatized affluence. Moreover, the quiet and polite xenophobia of the average Briton has been overlaid with explicit racism ranging from the ugly militancy of the National Front to the intellectualized prejudice of Enoch Powell. In the mid-1970s the National Front had gained in its minority support and attracted much publicity. In a by-election at Stechford in 1977, its candidate had 8.1 per cent of the votes cast (2,955 out of 36,240), beating the Liberal into fourth place.

All in all, then, the changing circumstances point to the need to develop a complex policy of integration.

Social inequality, conceived as differences in power and advantage, is the basic condition of the Black British. There is overwhelming evidence that the coloured population suffers discrimination on grounds of colour in employment, housing, leisure activities, and over the whole range of social relationships. Differences in power and advantage, whether based on colour or any other socially evaluated attribute, tend to be generalized and to be transmitted between generations. The social outlook for the coloured man is accordingly bleak. Whether he is admitted directly to citizenship through the immigration officer, or indirectly through an upbringing in Britain and through the school system, he typically has all the disadvantages of the lower levels of the native working class, as well as those of colour prejudice.

The effectiveness of the deliberate pursuit of equality through governmental action in the twentieth century has been severely limited in respect of the relative chances of the working class. In so far as the integration of Africans and Asians is thought of as a recapitulation of the gradual admission of the working class to full citizenship, the task calls for much more politically-forceful action than is embodied in the Race Relations Act of 1968 or 1976, or the mild gestures towards 'positive discrimination' which have been incorporated into the government's Urban Programme. Without such action, the position of the second and third generation of coloured people is likely to worsen. For example immigrant children generally have poorer educational performance (with all that this implies for later life chances) than natives. Children of West Indian antecedants, even with a full British schooling, have distributions which are 'negatively skewed' (that is, relatively large numbers with low scores) on all the measures of school attainment and, what is of the greatest significance, they do worse the more they are concentrated (as housing and employment policies force them to be) in predominantly working-class districts.

Obvious and persistent inequality, quite apart from its moral effectiveness, is a threatening source of conflict. In the context of class relations John Goldthorpe has analysed the paradox of the coexistence of gross inequality with a high degree of political consensus.[25] He divides the current explanations into two main types, 'social psychological' and 'culturalist'. I have discussed W. G. Runciman's contribution to the first type. What determines behaviour is not actual but *felt* deprivation. Limited imagination has served to integrate an unequal society. Goldthorpe's second type of analysis complements Runciman's. The British political culture is characterized by a balance 'that holds, even across lines of class and party, between participant, activist attitudes on the one hand, and acquiescent, passive attitudes on the other, between emotional commitment to political principle and cool pragmatism; between consensus on matters of procedure and conflict over particular issues'.[26] Socialization into the culture makes for apolitical and unfanatical citizens. In the past it has offered little basis for politically extremist egalitarian movements. Thus, as Runciman put it, 'there has been woven a social fabric in which traditional privilege blends with egalitarian socialism and class-consciousness with a veneration of existing institutions'.

Will race relations in Britain tear this fabric apart? Current conflict seems to open such a possibility. Goldthorpe uses the recent history of incomes policy to illustrate his argument that the distribution of incomes is not only, in the strict sense, unprincipled, but that there is little consensus on the principles which ought to be applied. He then goes on to argue that the normative reconstruction of economic life could, among other possibilities, be along the lines advocated by Lady Barbara Wooton in the 1950s in *The Social Foundations of Wages Policy*,[27] that is according to explicitly egalitarian principles. Race relations legislation is explicitly egalitarian. But the question remains of what responses are likely from those who are legally declared equal in an unequal society of conflicting interest groups, what economic and social costs will have to be paid for the absence of moral consensus, and what external controls will be required by those who prefer to maintain the *status quo*. The answers are far from comforting. In the autumn of 1976 *The Guardian* newspaper printed extracts from the Central Policy Review Staff Report on race relations, which was presented to the Labour Government in 1974 but never published. The Report stated:

There are uncomfortable parallels between the stiuation of Britain's coloured population and that of the Catholics in Northern Ireland. For fifty years British governments condoned discrimination and deprivation in Ulster, and in the end Ulster blew up in their face. We believe that not only for reasons of social justice but also to preserve social stability and order in the longer term more should be done to deal with the problems of race relations in this country.

What was needed, it said, was an attack on three fronts— against urban poverty, racial discrimination, and language disabilities. Such an approach would require extra money directed specifically at improving the situation of coloured minorities, particularly in the areas of housing, education, and employment. It also demanded a clear Government policy on race relations rather than mere declarations of principle. For, although successive Governments had declared their support for policies of positive discrimination, they had given no lead themselves in treating black and brown men as equivalent to whites.[28]

4   The rise of party

In this chapter I want to trace the development of deliberate organization in relation to the changing structure of class and status in Britain. I hinted in Chapter 3 at the fateful outcomes of the national political aims of Labour movements which were originally local in character. The story I now have to tell is first of the rise of working-class organization geared to the market and the state, second of the containment of these movements by a resourceful and adaptive Conservative Party, and third, of the incorporation of Labour leaders and what sociologists call the institutional segregation of industrial conflict. Finally, I will show that in the last decade industrial conflict has re-emerged with new developments in politics and economic management.

The Trade Unions and the Labour Party were the practical means of those whose weak market position could only be transcended by mobilizing their superior numbers both industrially and politically. Consideration of these twentieth-century movements of class, status, and party will lead to the conclusion that they had eventually to face the problem of 'alienation of the organizational apparatus from the membership'.[1] This fate befalls all large organizations. They tend to become remote from the interests they are created to serve, the more so the more successfully they recruit members. Thus Marx's remark that 'history is made behind men's backs' applies to those who consciously seek to change that history as much as to those who do not.

There is no more commonplace description of the twentieth century than the phrase, 'an age of organization'. If we pursue that phrase we also find as its corollaries the age of alienation and the age of anomie (or normlessness). I shall not cover the whole sweep of advancing organization, nor shall I more than refer to what Professor Finer has termed the *Anonymous Empire*[2] of pressure groups which lobby Westminster and Whitehall, and fill the gap between government and electorate between elections. There are many such interest groups. Some obscure and some ephemeral, some of long standing and widely known, they cover the whole gamut of social, economic, and political life. Confining examples to the first letter of the alphabet there is the Automobile Association, Aims of Industry, Amnesty, Alcoholics Anonymous, Action on Smoking and Health, and Associations of almost anyone anywhere ascertainable. My main concern, however, is with the central phenomenon of party in twentieth-century Britain—the rise of an organized working class and its consequences.

The more general background of the age of organization can be summarized as one in which more people are more involved in social relations beyond kinship at every stage of their lives. They work within an organization which is unlikely to be confined to their town or even their country. It is more and more likely to be a multinational company. Concurrently, within the contracting private sector of employment, there has been increasing concentration into a smaller number of larger firms. The invention of the limited company in the nineteenth century had paved the legal way for this development,[3] and sounded the knell of classical political economy as a valid theory applicable to the real world. Though at the beginning of the twentieth century the hundred largest companies still produced only 15 per cent of manufacturing output, today the hundred juggernauts of industry account for half the output, and the 90,000 firms with ten or fewer employees which were operating 70 years ago have been reduced to about 35,000.

In short, the organizations of production have expanded their range, reduced their numbers, and enlarged their scale. Married women have moved into paid employment, and what the Registrar General is pleased to call 'the economically active population' has steadily expanded both absolutely and proportionately, despite the parallel increase in the number of old and retired people. Leisure experiences, too, as well as work and education, are supplied by large-scale organizations, or take place in premises or with apparatus controlled by them. Even to watch television in the home is in fact to participate as a consumer in the final result of an enormous organizational effort. Similarly, in the case of children's play, the humble dandy is replaced by the skate-board, and juvenile prestige has come to depend less on skill with four old pram wheels and a few bits of wood and more on the ability to buy the most sophisticated and fashionable products of technology.

The largest organization is, of course, the State itself. In education, pre-schooling has increased, the years of compulsory attendance have been extended from effectively thirteen at the beginning of the century to sixteen now. The number of students remaining beyond the statutory leaving age has more than doubled in the last twenty years. The State also supplies cash, personnel, buildings, and other resources for a vast network of financial, personal, and social services. During the fifteen years from 1960 to 1975, the number of civilians employed by the central government rose by over 50 per cent, and local authority employees by over 60 per cent.

At the beginning of the century economic organizations were dominated by a private owning and controlling class, and political organizations by the Conservative and Liberal wings of the middle and upper classes. The Labour Party did not exist, and the Trade Union movement, though it had deep roots, especially among skilled workers, in the earlier stages of industrialism, was struggling to extend its organizational sway among semi-skilled and unskilled workers. There were two million union members at the beginning of this century, out of a total potential membership of nearly sixteen million. In other words, only one-eighth of all possible recruits had in fact been recruited. Put more technically, the density of membership was 13 per cent in 1900. This figure rose rapidly to reach 45 per cent by 1920. Since that date unionization has had fluctuating fortunes, but did not attain a higher density than it had in 1920 until the 1970s when, for the first time, it reached the present 50 per cent mark. The development of union density is shown in Graph 4.1. Unionization of women has always lagged behind that of men: so, too, has that of white-collar employees compared with manual workers. But since the Second World War, unionization of white-collar workers has increased very quickly. Thus while union membership among manual workers increased by only 0.9 per cent between 1948 and 1970, the increase among white-collar workers was 79.8 per cent. Nevertheless, the densities in 1970 were 53 per cent for manual workers, and 38 per cent for white-collar workers.[4]

Figure 4.1. Density of Union Membership 1901–1973

The end of the nineteenth century had brought the period of peaceful bourgeois domination to its late autumn of economic progress, imperial expansion, and national security. Political conflict divided contestants by religion more than class. But class politics were soon to sweep away the old divisions. The class struggles previously fought in an autonomous economic sphere were to enter into the political sphere, forcing governments to move from a passive 'keeping of the ring' into economic intervention and management. These movements towards a kind of 'Britain

incorporated' were essentially the consequences of developments in class structure, but the form they took, and particularly the part played in them by an organized working
class, was conditioned by those developments in the status
of citizenship which T. H. Marshall has analysed[5] —the civil
right to free association, out of which the Trade Unions
were built, and political enfranchisement, which gave the
Labour Party its opportunity.

These interconnected industrial and political movements
were, to be sure, class and collectivist organizations. But,
much more so than their counterparts in the continental
countries, their character was outstandingly social democratic in their commitment to the idea that opposition and
dissent were not merely tolerable but essential to a progressive society. Part of the explanation lies in the strong
historical link between the period of religious cleavage and
that of class cleavage in British politics. In its secular effect,
organized religion is usually and properly seen as primarily
an apparatus of social control. The 'heart of a heartless
world' as Marx acknowledged, but also, then a striking
phrase if now a cliché, 'the opiate of the people'.[6] In industrial Britain, the non-conformist chapels were the bearers not
only of religiosity but also of a radicalism which schooled
more than one generation of activists. Even the Church of
England nurtured its socialists—men like R. H. Tawney, or
Archbishop Temple, whose conception of the social order
began with the morality of the New Testament, and who
saw capitalism not simply as un-Christian, but anti-Christian
in that it converted economic means into overriding ends
and thus introduced the worship of false gods. I remember
as a child in the 1930s intoning the Magnificat at evensong
in a Northamptonshire church—'He hath put down the
mighty from their seat and hath exalted the humble and
meek.' And I vaguely assumed that the archaic language of
my elders had led them to essential truth but with wrong
tenses, just as they appeared also to be confused as to the
geographical location of Jerusalem.[7]

At all events, the religiously moulded inheritance of
native radicalism of the early years of this century was

responsible and respectable. It was a radicalism that accepted many traditional and middle-class values, not a radicalism of class warfare. It was therefore less terrifying to the dominant classes, making their resistance to the spread of political suffrage weaker and encouraging the political wing of the ruling class to stay as far as possible out of the battle between capital and labour in the work place—a policy in any case enjoined by nineteenth-century liberal theories of economics and politics. It gave working-class leaders to the twentieth century who, though tenaciously defensive of union interests in dealing with owners and managers, were anti-Marxist, non-revolutionary, pragmatic, and piecemeal in their reformist intentions.

At least until the 1960s there has been a marked asymmetry in the class relations of economics and politics in Britain—the one characterized by low and the other by high relations of trust. This asymmetry was formed out of a long history. Relations in the work place in industrial Britain reflected liberal doctrines of the market, defining labour as a commodity. The 'laws of market economics' provided an external 'scientific' substitute for ethical principles in the division of the fruits and declared that private charity rather than the employer was responsible for the mitigation of hardship, with the State as the ultimate but minimal provider when neither charity nor self-help prevented destitution. In the work place itself, the working class accepted the definitions imposed upon it by its economic masters. Collective bargaining resulted between employers enforcing a commodity conception of labour and a largely alienated work-force conditioned by the system into a zero-sum game conception of management/worker relations. As Alan Fox puts it: 'So far as work relations were concerned, the classes existed alongside each other, self-contained and independent; mutually alienated; the one seeking to protect itself against the superior power of the other by means of a process of low-trust bargaining.'[8]

Fox chooses his words carefully. He uses the phrase 'existed alongside', rather than 'confronted', because working-class independence ran only along certain dimensions of class relations. It was not an independence grounded in any generalized conception of class war in the Marxist sense.

Indeed it could be argued that the working-class independence that expressed itself through Trade Unionism, collective bargaining, and the sub-culture which celebrated solidarity and collectivism, was only conceded legal status and . . . social acceptance by the more powerful groups in society because working-class independence showed clear signs of limiting itself to relatively marginal challenges of a bread-and-butter kind at the work place.[9]

Political relations were able to rest more directly on social bonds outside the work place that were strongly antithetical to doctrines of class struggle. That is why it can be reasonably argued that the norms of political attitudes were ones of high trust by contrast with the established and enduring low-trust industrial relations.

Paradoxically, the General Strike of 1926, which may reasonably be described as a moment of tense confrontation between the two main classes, also provided unmistakable evidence of a consensual political culture. The stories of good humour and fair play between strikers and soldiers have since taken their place in national mythology. I am not thinking of those, but rather of the exchanges in the House of Commons and in Downing Streeet before and after the event between the Conservative Prime Minister, Stanley Baldwin, and the Labour members. The year before the strike, two Tories (one a Conservative Trade Unionist) put down a Private Members' Bill to end the political contribution to the Labour Party from Trade Union dues. The Bill would probably have succeeded, but Baldwin opposed it. After discoursing on the growing power of the organized employers and organized workers, and on the tradition of letting Englishmen develop their own associations in their own way, he went on as follows:

We find ourselves, after these two years in power, in possession of the greatest majority our party ever had . . . because, rightly or wrongly, we succeeded in creating the impression that we stood for stable Government and for peace in the country between all classes of the community . . . I want my party today to make a gesture to the country . . . and to say to them: We have our majority; we believe in the justice of this Bill . . . but we are going to withdraw

our hand; we are not going to push our political advantage home.
Although I know that there are those who work for different ends
from most of us in this House, yet there are many in all ranks and
in all parties who will re-echo my prayer: 'Give Peace in our time,
O Lord'.[10]

Fourteen years later David Kirkwood, described by G. M.
Young as 'once the firebrand of Clydeside', wrote a letter
to Baldwin remarking the change in attitudes between 1914
and 1938. In it he said 'it seemed to me . . . that in your
speech you made flesh the feelings of us all, that the antagonism, the bitterness, the class rivalry, were unworthy,
and that understanding and amity were possible'.[11]

We are listening here to two characteristic voices of
British politics even after the organized working class had
become the major opposition party. Disraeli's one-nation
Toryism and social-democratic Labour were those two
voices. The hard heads of right and left poured scorn on
them then, and still do today. It is easy to dismiss them as
rhetorical sentimentalists. It is wiser perhaps to recognize
that the creation of universal suffrage, and all the apparatus
of industrial bargaining and conciliation, also entailed the
creation of vested interests in them for both classes.

Alternatively, these British political peculiarities have
been explained by the thesis of a deferential working class.
On this there is a large literature.[12] The point of departure
of the thesis is that, extension of the suffrage notwithstanding, a country with a hugely preponderent proletarian
electorate has returned more Conservative than Labour
governments. Even if we start from 1918, so as to ignore
the early period of Labour Party formation and the still
restricted male franchise, the party of the working class
has held office for only nineteen of the subsequent sixty
years.

This comparative electoral failure cannot be explained
away by denying the proposition that Labour has been the
working-class party. The Communist Party has never attracted more than a fraction of 1 per cent of votes,[13] and
the decline of the Liberals after their split in 1916 took
more Liberal voters into the Conservative than into the

Labour camp. Between the Wars the class base of the Labour party took a long time to establish. Consolidation came only with the Second World War when there was a profound national shift of political outlook which led to the Labour landslide of 1945. The share of the vote at General Elections taken by Labour is shown in Figure 4.2. Even so, the capture of the working class as a potentially overwhelming political force was never complete. Labour electoral support levelled off after the Second World War to leave the two main parties in fine balance.

Figure 4.2. Labour's Share of the Vote. General Elections 1900–1974

Between the Wars, the Labour Party increasingly attracted the loyalties of working men and their wives, partly at the expense of the Liberals and the Conservatives, but most of all among those families with no history of party allegiance. Nevertheless, a large residue of cross-voting, that is, voting for the party of the other class, remained, and it is at this point that interest in the Tory-voting worker becomes salient. As Butler and Stokes put it, there was

one grand historical paradox: the first major nation of the world to become industrialized, a nation in which 70 per cent of the people regard themselves as working-class, has regularly returned Conservative Governments to power. Between 1886 and 1964 the

Conservative Party was defeated by decisive majorities only twice—in 1906 and 1945. Such a record could only have been achieved through heavy 'defection' to the Conservatives among the industrial working class . . . the working-class elector was likelier than the middle-class elector to support the party of the opposite class.[14]

This is true, at least on a generous definition of the working class—and incidentally crucial for the survival of the Conservative Party in the period we are discussing. In 1970, the Conservatives took 45 per cent of their votes from manual workers. Nevertheless, it is also true, and no less important, that in that same year the manual-worker vote between Labour and Conservative was 64 per cent to 36 per cent. At first glance, these figures appear to contradict one another—the one showing Conservative success in attracting nearly half of its votes from manual workers, and the other showing that nearly two-thirds of manual workers vote for their natural party. They are, in fact, the same figures put in two different ways as answers to two different questions. If we ask where parties *get* their votes, we find that the Tories get 45 per cent of them from the working class. But if we ask where the classes *send* their votes, we find that only 36 per cent of them send them to the Tories. The difference is due simply to the fact that the working class is larger than the middle class.

The slow growth and limited success of the Labour Party as the political organization of the working class is therefore to be explained partly by its relatively late start, partly by the inevitably slow process of building up loyalty as parents passed on their party commitment to their children, and partly from the brilliant ingenuity of the Conservative Party in rebutting the twentieth-century assumption that political parties should be seen solely in terms of class interest. It is the success of the Conservatives in combating this one-dimensional view of politics, and the corresponding failure of Labour to maximize its appeal to class that accounts for British electoral history, not the deferential working-class Tory voter. Such voters are, of course, to be found: and those manual workers who vote Conservative are more likely to be strong supporters of the monarchy than are their workmates who vote Labour. But before the inference is accepted that the working-class Tory vote is deferential, we must also notice that more than half of the working-class *Labour* voters are royalists, and that monarchist sentiment is more common among the Labour-voting working class than among the Labour-voting middle class.

We are dealing here, to be sure, with only one indicator of what writers have in mind in defining deferential voting: but weighing all the evidence we are forced back to Walter Bagehot's judgement that the English *as a nation* are deferential. We have no need to ascribe these attributes exclusively to the Tory working class.

The incomplete but steady consolidation of party loyalties continued for over half a century. During the last decade, however, the situation has become unstable. The apparent electoral balance is caused primarily by the persistence of voting habits formed in youth. Clues to future development among those most recently reaching voting age point in a different direction. A study by Phyllis Thorburn confirms earlier suggestions that in the 1960s the association between class and party began to wane.[15] It is difficult to distinguish between generational and life-cycle effects in these matters, and important to do so since it is well established that party loyalty tends to increase with age. However, from a study of men in England and Wales in 1972, Thorburn confirms the view put forward by Butler and Stokes that class polarization began to diminish in the 1960s. She suggests, however, that the process has not been symmetrical. Labour appears to have maintained its position as the party of the working class, while middle-class radicalism has begun to threaten the Conservatives.

The weakening of class alignment has been accompanied by other changes in electoral behaviour which may also help to explain it. Voting turn-out declined from 84 per cent in 1950 to 72 per cent in 1970, and the fall was especially heavy in traditional Labour strongholds. The electorate became more volatile. Unprecedented swings began to appear from the later 1950s, especially in by-elections. The swings in the General Elections in the 1960s were more than twice as great as those of the 1950s, and the opinion polls returned evidence of even more violent and sudden shifts of opinion. The hold of the two main parties was weakening, though remaining evenly balanced. Fitful Liberal revivals took place and, which may turn out to be of greater significance for the future of class politics, the Scottish and Welsh Nationalists gained rapidly in the 1970s to secure the election of candidates in the General Election of October 1974.

So the full story of the rise of party organization along class lines in twentieth-century Britain must also comprehend the beginning of its displacement from the centre of party politics and perhaps even its eventual demise.

In Chapter 2, I was at pains to juxtapose two contradictory features of British economic development—the persistence of inequality, and the growth of affluence. Affluence has unquestionably made the stronger impact on popular political perceptions. Post-war prosperity, continuing late into the 1960s, gradually established expectations of annual increments of income and welfare, with the political parties increasingly seen less as class organizations than as competing instrumentalities—a competition, incidentally, in which Macmillan was at least as adept as Gaitskell in the eyes of ordinary voters. And intellectual fashion supported popular opinion. There was, in the 1950s, a confirmed confidence in Keynesian economic management. Full employment seemed to be assured by it, and bitter memories of the slump years could be dismissed as irrelevant relics of a banished society.

Indeed in the pink glow of 'Butskellism', and the politics of the centre ground, inequality was difficult to discern. The traditional call to uneasy conscience from the survey traditions of Booth and Rowntree seemed to have ended with the last short book published by Rowntree in 1951.[16] It told us that the percentage of the working class who were in poverty, which had been nearly one-third in 1936, was now reduced in 1950 to less than 3 per cent. And the triumph was attributable to Keynesian full employment. Poverty was no longer a class phenomenon. Indeed it was widely regarded as no phenomenon at all, and had to be rediscovered in the 1960s.

Ironically in those years, Labour Party intellectuals, even at a time when the class alignment of voting had gone as far as it ever did, became more than half convinced that the social base of their party support was being eroded by embourgeoisment—the assimilation of the working class into the life and manners of the middle class. The famous study of Luton workers by a group of Cambridge dons[17] dealt severely with this doctrine and called instead for a new and determined political leadership of the Labour Party. The Cambridge dons got no response from the Labour leaders, but meanwhile the 1964 election left no-one prepared to argue further the crude form of the embourgeoisment thesis with them. In retrospect, what was most telling in Goldthorpe and Lockwood's study was the identification of *privatization* among the relatively prosperous new working class, and of *instrumentalism* in the work place among employees of all classes. Affluent workers were becoming more privatized in that they sought the good life more at home with their wives and families than at work or in the traditional male organizations of the pub and club. And all employees were becoming instrumental in that they increasingly regarded unions, politics, and work not as ends in themselves but as means to private ends. The unionization of white-collar employees is the story of a principle treasured by the working class—collectivism—disseminated to other classes, but at the same time made instrumental. In the process the Trade Unions began to lose their class character, if not their class rhetoric. Even the Association of First Division Civil Servants is now affiliated to the T.U.C.

Where embourgeoisment *had* taken place was not in the rank and file, but among the political leaders of the organized working class. The social composition of the Labour benches and cabinets had undergone a striking transformation. Between the Wars 72 per cent of Labour MPs came from rank-and-file employment, and 15 per cent were university graduates. By 1945 only half came from the working class, and by 1970 only one-quarter, by which time the proportion of graduates had risen to more than half. Among cabinet ministers the trend was even more striking. In MacDonald's 1924 cabinet, 30 per cent were graduates. In 1969 under Wilson, the graduates made up 83 per cent.

These changes in the social antecedents of Labour leaders do not, of course, demonstrate subversion of working-class interest. It is what men do, not where they come from, on which that question has to be settled. What the statistics do indicate, however, is a gradual change in the image presented to the electorate. In the case of Labour politicians, that image is now far from proletarian, whether revolutionary or gradualist. In a more literal sense, the television image further emphasizes the common social personalities of Labour and Conservative party leaders. Television is *par excellence* the centre ground over which the parties squabble, and they do so decorously, reinforcing an indistinguishable impression of alternative teams of natural governors.

In parallel with these developments, participation in local Labour parties has become pathetically weak. Since 1952 the individual membership of the Labour Party has fallen continuously. It had risen to a peak of over one million in 1950. But by 1976 it had declined, even on official returns, to two-thirds of that figure, and on other estimates was as low as a quarter of a million.[18] On the basis of individual party membership per hundred party voters, Labour is now numerically among the smallest socialist parties in Western Europe.[19] In short, the increasing incorporation of the Labour Party at the national centre of power has been accompanied by a spectacular decline of participation by members in local organizations.

What, then, has become of working-class interests, or indeed of any interest officially pursued by national parties and nationally-organized unions? There are two, apparently contradictory, answers—national corporatism, and fragmented localism. Certainly changes in the structure of politics, as distinct from electoral behaviour, have been of great significance in the 1960s and '70s. The previous conditions, before the Second World War, of relatively weak trade unionism and high unemployment, and after the War of economic growth and unambitious unionism, were essentially ones which allowed the market to regulate industrial conflict. But the more recent conditions of economic stagnation, inflation, and strong unionism have forced the state into new forms of elaborate intervention. Institutional segregation of industrial conflict has been breaking down. Instead the economy has become increasingly politicized, and governments have sought to substitute their own regulation for that of the market. Ironically, it is the political Right that supports this new statism, and the political Left which demands free market bargaining. The T.U.C. leaders are increasingly caught in the cross-fire of sectional and national interest, and their Labour Party counterparts in office are the frequently embarrassed guardians not of working-class interests but of the nation's. Politically, party leaders have been forced into a curious schizophrenia. Political decisions are increasingly diverted from the traditional rhetoric of party debate, and the locus of politics has shifted away from parliament to the negotiations of government with organized economic interest. Hence the spectre is raised of an emerging corporate state, the absorption, that is, of all interests into a single and hierarchical political organization.

On the other hand, the rise of locally based direct action groups is also a marked feature of the past decade. They are, at least in part, a response to the alienation of leaders from members in organizations of massive scale. In the work place, these forces have contributed to the increasing power of shop stewards. In consequence, the capacity of the T.U.C. to maintain agreements with Labour or Conservative Chancellors has been undermined. Control over the membership by the Union leaders, who represent them in the corporatist negotiations with government, is just as uncertain as is that of the C.B.I. over its 12,000 member companies and 200 trade and employer associations. Wages and even local plant management are determined on the local shop floor, and not by conversations in Westminster. This is one powerful reason why observers like Alan Fox refuse to accept current fashionable warnings of the imminent coming of a British corporate State. The continuance of low-trust relations in the direct dealings of shop stewards and plant managers is the principal manifestation of the class struggle. What Fox describes as 'arms-length contractual bargaining' is deeply ingrained: on the one hand, it is a defence against corporatism; on the other hand, it holds little prospect for industrial democracy because such a development requires managers and employees to pursue efficiency together in something other than a zero-sum game.

Alienation from the state apparatus is an equally widespread popular experience. Bureaucracy, like bourgeoisie, serves more often as a term of abuse than as a descriptive category. Hardly a day passes without the newspapers complaining about this ugly polysyllable. *The Times* reporting, in August 1976, a new book by Gordon Tullock,[20] described it as a 'comprehensive criticism of politicians and civil servants for being more interested in feathering their own nests than serving the public'. Professor Tullock argues that civil servants are just like other men and that therefore 'they will make most of their decisions in terms of what benefits them, not society as a whole'. And, 'as a general rule, a bureaucrat will find that his [interests are best served] . . . if the bureaucracy in which he works expands'.

A few days later the newspapers announced that the two large Civil Service unions, alarmed by what their leaders described as a 'hate campaign against civil servants', had distributed a pamphlet to MPs and other Unions defending the incumbents of public offices against exaggerated rumours of their pay and pensions, and against misrepresentation of their conduct towards citizens. The Civil Service Unions had also protested against cuts in public expenditure in general and public service jobs in particular. No one ought to need reminding that forced unemployment is a private tragedy and a public failure, but anyone could be forgiven, after reading or watching the news in 1976, for thinking that there had been a sharp reduction in the

number of officials, if not from the arrival of the Conservative Government of 1970, then at least since Mr. Healey's.
And this would be specially marked in the case of local
government with its alleged reorganization for greater economy and efficiency. In fact the opposite is the case.

The Manpower Watch Survey—made jointly by central
and local government—records that, between March
1975 and March 1976—a much publicized 'No Growth'
period—there was an *increase* in English and Welsh local
government staff of over 30,000. On a longer view it is clear
that Governments of either colour preside over continuous
bureaucratic growth. There were a million and a quarter
local government employees in 1960. It was two million
when Labour displaced the Tories in 1964. They added
over 400,000 before the Conservatives came back in 1970
determined to turn the tide. But the tide flowed on. By
1975 there were 2,875,000 despite the fact that 77,000
were transferred to the N.H.S. and Water Services in 1974
and so did not appear in the 1975 total. No wonder that
the National Association of Local Government Officers is
the fourth largest union in the country.

Taking a still wider view it can be seen that in the twentieth century the occupational structure has shifted its
centre of gravity from basic productive employment to the
tertiary sector of services and administration. One measure
of the change is that between 1911 and 1966 white-collar
numbers went up 176 per cent, while manual jobs rose only
5 per cent and actually decreased after 1931.

These figures reflect an increasingly organized world in
which bureaucracy is the dominant working principle.
Though the word 'community' also spatters its pages, the
contemporary newspaper habitually looks out, sees organizations everywhere, and tells us in a more or less sensation-
alist way how people enter them in pursuit of their interest
only to lose themselves. Paul Johnson, in the *New Statesman*[21] provides a characteristic expression of this view with
an attack of spectacular verbal violence on the leaders of
the T.U.C. For Johnson this organizational élite are the
greatest threat to democracy in modern times and the

closed shop the greatest blow against freedom in his life time.

It is the thesis of the bureaucratic brothers that they represent the people; that what they are doing, in erecting their private empires, in extending their bureaucratic control and grabbing jobs for their boys, in remorselessly driving their juggernaut over the prostrate bodies of individual men and women, that all this is done by, with, for and in the name of the people. Jack Jones, who might well be described as the Louis XIV of the trade union takeover, has seemingly convinced himself that 'Le peuple, c'est moi!' . . . But all the available evidence suggests that, at a time when so many members of the Establishment—ministers and MPs, dons and civil servants, experts and publicists—are hurrying to pay their respects to the new totalitarianism, and sell their shares in individual liberty, the ordinary decent people of Britain are strongly opposed to rule by trade-union bureaucrats.

In common speech, of course, the word 'bureaucracy' is an established term of abuse. The word 'bureau' referred originally to the cloth covering the desks of French government officials in the eighteenth century. With its suffix added it came to refer to the rule of government, and a host of '-ocracies' have since been added to the vocabulary of politics as commentators have searched desperately to find the ultimate seat of power in modern society. The pejorative term then spread throughout Europe during the nineteenth century, at first to ridicule the high-handed arrogance of officials in absolutist regimes, and later more generally as a whip for the backs of unresponsive organizations, tortuous methods of administration, and large-scale enterprizes (whether of government, business, religion, or recreation) in which power was concentrated into the hands of the administrative few.

There is, on the other hand, a technical, social-scientific use of bureaucracy to describe a type of social organization deliberately devised by men for the rational and efficient pursuit of defined purposes. The classic source for the analysis of bureaucracy in non-evaluative terms is the German sociologist, Max Weber, who wrote at the end of the nineteenth and in the early part of the twentieth century. No one saw more clearly than he that bureaucracy and large-scale organization were the fundamental phenomena of modern political, social, and economic life. And Weber's account of bureaucracy, from one point of view, reminds us of its virtues. Bureaucracy, he noted, was distinguished from other forms of human authority and control by its routinized rationality, its capacity to attain a high degree of efficiency, its stability, the stringency of its discipline, and its reliability. It is a matter of national pride in Britain that it showed the world how to escape from the corrupt control of administration by the privileged into uncorrupt and dedicated public service recruited on merit in open competition, by the Northcote-Trevelyan and Gladstonian reforms; and that was the acceptable face of bureaucracy.

It is true that Weber at the same time saw the tragedy of the highly organized world into which industrialization would take us—a world of disenchantment, robbed of magic and mystery. Even charisma, the gift of grace, would be routinized within it and freedom and individuality could be destroyed by it. Nevertheless, in company with both the Leftists and the Rightests of his age, Weber identified modernity with the spread of bureaucratic administration:

This is true of church and state, of armies, political parties, economic enterprizes, organizations to promote all kinds of causes, private associations, clubs, and many others. However many forms there may be which do not appear to fit this pattern, such as collegial representative bodies, parliamentary committees, soviets, honorary officers, lay judges, and what-not, and however much people may complain about the 'evils of bureaucracy', it would be sheer illusion to think for a moment that continuous administrative work can be carried out in any field except by means of officials working in offices. The whole pattern of everyday life is cut to fit this frame-work. For bureaucratic administration is, other things being equal, always from a formal technical point of view, the most rational type. For the needs of mass administration today, it is completely indispensable. The choice is only that between bureaucracy and dilettantism in the field of administration.[22]

Adherents of different ideological traditions than that of Weber's liberalism echoed his celebration of the inevitable march of bureaucracy as well as his ambivalence towards it. Sheldon Wolin[23] has written a subtle and scholarly account of the origin of this view in all political camps. Whatever differences there were in diagnosis and prescription, most of the major writers have been agreed on the general formula for developing wealth, welfare, and social order–organization. Thus for the nineteenth-century French conservative, de Maistre, the organization of society into a vast hierarchy of authority would reinstitute stability and peace under the command of king and pope, assisted by a public-spirited aristocracy. For his compatriot, Auguste Comte, there would be an organized hierarchy of savant-priests. For yet another compatriot, Emile Durkheim, the organization of society had to be on the basis of professional and producing groups. For the proponents of managerial élitism in the twentieth century the best organization of society is one under the control of the professional managers and administrators who alone possess the requisite knowledge for maintaining social equilibrium in the age of successive technological revolutions.

Weber himself remorselessly drove home the inference from the indispensibility of bureaucracy that it made no difference whether an economic system was organized on a capitalist or a socialist basis. And he adds:

> though by no means alone, the capitalistic system has undeniably played a major role in the development of bureaucracy. Indeed, without it capitalistic production could not continue and any rational type of socialism would simply have to take it over and increase its importance. Its development, largely under capitalistic auspices, has created an urgent need for stable, strict, intensive, and calculable administration. It is this need which gives bureaucracy a crucial role in our society as the central element in any kind of any large-scale administration.[24]

Bureaucracy, I would stress, in theories of the Right and the Left, has been seen as an instrument not only for efficiency but also of social control. There is accordingly an élitism of the Left as well as of the Right. Lenin is perhaps the outstanding example. In Professor Wolin's phrase 'organization was to mass in Lenin's theory what idea had been to matter in Plato's: that which imparted form to the formless'. Lenin was the first to seize the implications of transferring politics to the plane of organization.

He taught that politics had meaning only within an organizational setting. The trick was not to destroy the political but to absorb it into organization to create a new compound. The irony is that his prescription for revolution has also been used to preserve giant capitalism. Democracy has no meaning in such élitist thought except in so far as it is consonant with the imperatives of organization. Thus Lenin wrote:

> Bureaucracy *versus* democracy is the same thing as centralism *versus* (local) democracy as opposed to the organizational principle of the opportunists of Social Democracy. The latter want to proceed from the bottom upwards . . . The former proceed from the top, and advocate the extension of the rights and powers of the centre in respect of the parts . . . My idea is 'bureaucratic' in the sense that the Party is built from the top downwards . . .[25]

Lenin's theory was the basis for Communist organization. But the historical roots of British socialism were never like that. Democracy came to Britain from the bottom upwards. The urban working classes of the nineteenth century were uprooted newcomers to the growing provincial industrial towns who responded to their circumstances with extraordinary social inventiveness to give Britain in the first half of the twentieth century its most characteristic popular organizations—the Cooperative store, the Trade Union, and the Labour Party, as well as the dance hall, the football club, and the Friendly Society. The first and the greatest three of these were experiments in democracy. This urban proletariat created its own local, communal welfare societies. Nothing could have been more democratic than the constitution of the Co-op, nothing more fraternal than the Miners' Lodge. Nowhere could we find a more sturdy institutional protection for individuals against becoming a mass to be manipulated. Then, with political organization as its instrument, the Labour movement set out to nationalize democracy and welfare; to translate fraternity, equality, and liberty from the local community to the national state.

What has been the outcome? In 1973, very near to the end of his life, R.H.S. Crossman gave an account, in the form of a review, of the Labour movement as he had experienced it. It was in essence a lament for the eclipse of voluntarism by bureaucratic organization—a disappointment in Westminster and a despair in Whitehall:

From the 1920s on, the normal left-wing attitude has been opposed to middle-class philanthropy, charity, and everything else connected with do-gooding. Those of us who became socialists grew up with the conviction that we must in this point ally ourselves with the professionals and the trade unions and discourage voluntary effort particularly since it was bound to reduce the number of jobs available to those in need.

I am now convinced that the Labour Party's opposition to philanthropy and altruism and its determined belief in economic self-interest as the driving dynamic of society has done it grievous harm. For ironically enough the Party, trade unions, and the Co-operative were all a hundred years ago inspired by a profound and passionate altruism—a belief in a new Jerusalem—linked with an urgent sense of duty—a conviction that it was an essential part of socialism to practise what one preached by volunteering to help comrades in distress.[26]

So the movement which had invented the social forms of modern participatory democracy and practised them in Union Branch and Co-op meeting, thereby laying a Tocquevillian foundation for democracy, was ironically fated to develop through its political party the threats of a bureaucratic state. So much is this so now that when Norman Dennis protests against these emerging tyrannies with the authentic voice of a deeply-rooted English socialism, he is heard with approval by Sir Keith Joseph, and dismissed as a nuisance by the Labour establishment. Mr. Dennis has written, for example, a completely convincing demolition of British planning practices, from the standpoint of democratic socialism in the English tradition which I have described.[27]

Planning is, of course, associated with left-wing politics and the illogical 'therefore' is frequently added that criticism of it is comfort to the Right. But the 'hidden hand' is also 'a planner' with the market as its instrument. This form of 'planning', however, is vitiated by unequal distributions of power, wealth, and income between citizens; it does not accurately reflect the preferences of citizens in community as opposed to individuals in a market. Studies

of planning do often turn out to be a more or less sophisticated attack on socialism and a plea to 'return to the
market'. With Mr. Dennis, however, the criticism is directed
to the planner's indifference to egalitarian notions of income and power, and his ignorance of the preferences and
values of the community he is appointed to serve.

On what grounds can we accept or reject the theory or
principle by which a bureaucracy is guided in its action?
Sociologists call these grounds the 'legitimation' of the
organization and its activities. Max Weber pointed out that
organizations differ greatly when they come to decide
whether what they are doing is 'morally right' and based
upon 'the correct and relevant data'. One type of organization accepts the word of its leader on both these matters.
This is charisma, the personal authority of the inspired
leader. *Ipse dixit*—the sayings of the leader are the criteria
of both truth and worth. A second type of organization
rests its activities upon a piety for what has actually, alleg-
edly, or presumably always existed and upon a belief in
the everyday routine as being the inviolable norm of conduct. This is organized authority based on tradition. Thirdly,
there are organizations to which Weber gave the term
bureaucratic, which appeal to the rule of general laws applying to all within the jurisdiction of the organization
without regard to differences of race, age, family background, or social condition. The legitimacy of such an
organization's authority does not depend upon the actual
benefits given to particular persons, but upon the legality
of the general rule which has been purposely thought out
and enacted. Authority here is based on formal as distinct
from substantive justice.

This said, it is immediately apparent how enormously
ambitious is the claim, scientific and moral, for a bureaucratic organization.

The task is relatively easy, and successful bureaucratic
routine administrations have emerged, where the same
service can (and especially where it must) be provided day
after day in an identical way to large numbers of people.
This is the case with, for example, gas, water, and electricity

supplies, and transport and postal services. Bureaucratic administration is also appropriate, if more problematic, in the production of houses when, because of chronic shortage, large numbers of identical dwellings must be produced. It may even be appropriate to the demolition of houses where a few formal characteristics—for example, whether the house is at all damp, or possibly where a measurable amount of dampness is present—enable an official to distinguish unequivocally between a slum house and a non-slum house. But when we come to the service of more subtle and varied human needs in medicine, social security, or education, difficulties multiply and a fourth type of legitimation appears which is increasingly important in the modern world. The activities of an organization are not 'proved' right and good because they are the command of a charismatic leader, or because of tradition, or because they can be subsumed under some general rule, but because they are so certified by the trained members of the organization whose special function it is to evaluate the particular issue. This is professional authority. Decisions, characteristically in the form of 'advice', are made by those who have been appointed to a 'sphere of competence' on the basis of qualifications attested by a professional group of peers.

As long as the group of professionals make claims only in the technical sphere, and as long as they merely say 'this is the given task, we know the most economical means of accomplishing it', the organization will show many acceptable bureaucratic characteristics. But it is also possible for professionals to make claims in such a way, or to such an extent, that their legitimation resembles that of the inspired leader. These claims to legitimation typically take the form of a kind of group charisma. Each case is adjudicated not by an appeal to strictly formal conceptions unambiguously established, made public, and safely recorded 'in the files', but by informal judgements rendered by the personal incumbent of the professional status in terms of concrete ethical or practical valuations. These valuations may be quite opaque to those outside the profession. The professional, by definition, is absolved from justifying his decision; he does not need to reveal his basis in theory or fact or value.

Thus the legitimacy of professional bureaucratic decisions must be judged in two ways. The first is scientific. Decisions ought to be made in the light of ascertainable knowledge. No one can read Mr. Dennis's account of planning in Sunderland and retain confidence in the professionalism of planners. Nor is this an isolated local example. Here, speaking more generally, and with examples from many branches of public policy, is R. H. S. Crossman again:

> But I was even more worried, particularly when I became a Minister and was able to see a good deal for myself, by the inexplicable decisions under which I found our social services to be operating, decisions which in themselves were inhuman and stupid. And yet as I knew full well they had been made by intelligent, well-intentioned people. How could it be possible that now we had abolished the amateurism of philanthropy and placed the administration of our welfare state in highly professional hands such decisions could be made?[28]

The second way of judging professional bureaucracies emphasizes the capacity of ordinary people to reach rational decisions about matters which directly affect them. But even more it emphasizes the moral proposition that the exercise of personal discretion is itself a social and personal good. When such discretion has to be abbreviated, as is unavoidable on countless grounds, the case of those who desire to impose restrictions must be well based in fact and convincing in terms of political, social, and moral argument. Otherwise we are all too likely to forget, in a fog of pseudo science, that, as Mr. Dennis likes to say, 'the citizen is usually his own best expert'.

The outlook, some may conclude, is gloomy—the huge private businesses we have created, and the public servants we invented to realize justice, freedom, and equity will become our tyrannical masters. Even the Ombudsman will turn out to be another professional bureaucrat.

What, then, is to be done? The characteristic response by the centre to peripheral unrest is further efforts at incorporation. The various forms of community development projects, initiated and controlled from Whitehall under the

Urban Programme, exemplify the pattern. Central direction is resented by local activists. For example, the grand national design for developing and applying a response to poverty through more effectively delivered and integrated local social services degenerates into a complicated pattern of conflict between the centre and the locality, and within the locality between competing interest groups. It would be idle to pretend to an easy answer. But if there are answers, they might more readily be found in our own heritage of democracy and socialism. Our hard-won civil liberites need new defence from a radical overhaul of administrative laws. We have an unfinished programme of greater economic and social equality. But the fraternity which underpins it all cannot survive the national organization we have erected . Such a scale only generates Robert Michels's 'Iron Law of Oligarchy'. Weber saw only one escape from bureaucratic tyranny—a return to small scale. Subsequent writers following this line have been dismissed as proposing economic absurdity as did William Morris in *News From Nowhere,* or medieval romanticism as did G. K. Chesterton in *The Napoleon of Notting Hill Gate.* We shall return to these issues in my final chapter.

Meanwhile, to sum up three-quarters of a century of organizational development: we have witnessed the massive development of working-class political and industrial combination, and a parallel response by the dominant classes through the Conservative Party and the employers' associations. In this sense, we have seen the rise of party; and between them they have created a vast proliferation of the organs of state. We have also seen the rise of a host of sectional interest groups about which I have said little. As a whole, these developments amount to an organizational revolution. But it has been no revolution in the Marxist sense. Certainly the working class became consciously organized, industrially and politically, in the first two decades of the century, and certainly some of its members envisaged social ends inspired by the Russian revolution. After the First World War, many poor families who had voted Tory when first admitted to the franchise, were drawn not to

Liberal but to Labour allegiance. Older men might grumble
that before the War there was, as one put it, 'very little o'
that clap-trap about profit an' t' bosses an' Socialism an'
there being no God . . . Now everyon's at it'.[29] Fellow-
travelling was fashionable in small intellectual circles,[30]
and the Webbs thought of Russia as a new civilization.[31]
But no serious Leninist vanguard movement ever emerged.
Class struggle was muted and fragmented.

The main consequence of the rise of the working-class
party was national incorporation of its leaders—a development as unanticipated by its pioneers as it was intended by
the liberal-minded elements of the upper and middle classes.
Over the following half century, a new Establishment was
welded together and supported by the vested interests not
only of the traditionally powerful, but also of the new
men of power who now also stood to lose by any departure
into radical adventures from the established framework of
industrial bargaining and parliamentary procedure. And
these convergent interests always had popular support.
Class was never the sole dimension of life as subjectively
experienced by ordinary people. It had its place in politics
and the Labour Party came to occupy that place: but it
was limited by rising affluence and mobility, and by localism as well as nationalism—both entrenched sentiments
which enabled Conservatives to hang on to a vital segment
of votes across the class divide. 'My country Right or Left'
was not only Orwell's instinct in the early days of the
Second World War: it was also a national disposition.

Yet organizational decay was eventually the price that
had to be paid for incorporation. The Labour leaders who
set out to conquer national politics could not have anticipated either their metropolitan success, or their later provincial failure. Local Labour Parties now are even more
deserted than the chapels to which they owed so much of
their early education. The mass membership is alienated
and inert.

Meanwhile, after the Second World War there was a gradual consolidation of Trade Union strength under conditions of full employment. The market continued to be the

regulator of both political and industrial relations until the mid-sixties. Since then, economic stagnation and inflation have together created a new situation which we can describe as the spread of politics into the economy. Unions have become more militant and extended their organization far beyond the industrial proletariat. The state has become less parliamentary and more the centre of attempts to incorporate and pacify competing economic interests—all of whom are recalcitrant corporatists. And localized conflict is rife. The old struggles have shifted back to the work place and the locality where they began, and where horizons are narrowest and objectives most limited and sectional.

A heroic age of universalist political controversy has ended. Freedom, the truly precious inheritance, is preserved. Equality has been displaced by a political search for economic growth: and the problem of fraternity is still with us.

5 Between the generations

'WHAT the few have today the many will demand tomorrow.' That is Professor Daniel Bell's summary of the social history of industrial society.[1] Michael (now Lord) Young and Peter Willmott have called it the principle of stratified diffusion and turned it into a metaphor. They picture successive ranks of families in Britain drawn up in a column of social class, but a column on the march. 'The last rank keeps its distance from the first and the distance between them does not lessen. But as the column advances, the last rank does eventually reach and pass the point which the first rank passed some time before.'[2]

With this metaphor in mind, let us look back for a moment to the beginning of the century. Here is G. M. Young remembering the coronation year of 1902,[3] when he was an Oxford undergraduate:

We looked forward to living, with some improvements, the sort of life our fathers had lived. By *we* I do not mean the wealthy classes but the sort of people who filled the public schools and the two ancient universities, not rich, but comfortably off, who took games, books, and hospitality for granted: sons of lawyers, civil servants, MPs: young men who might succeed to their father's share in some old family business, or seek an outlet for their energies in India, or the Sudan, with Cromer for their ideal, and Milner for their example. It was an attractive life, I think we might say the most attractive that European civilization had ever fashioned for itself, and the prospect of living that life and transmitting it to our sons and daughters was an incentive, I should judge, more powerful than any quest for wealth or power. In a word, and it was a word often spoken in those days, England was a very good country for gentlemen. And it all rested on two things—an income tax so moderate that it was hardly felt: and an unlimited supply of cheap and efficient domestic service. Pull those pillars down, and that social hierarchy topples. That also we could not foresee.

That was the England of G. M. Young's youth. But at the same time, some two hundred miles further north in the same country, Robert Roberts was growing up in industrial working-class England, and tells of how his elders told him

of a man with a large family struggling to keep his sick father with them. At last the old man insisted he should be taken to the work-house. They set off, the wife picking up his few belongings, and the father on his son's back. *En route* they stopped to rest a while on a stone seat. 'It was here', said the old man, 'I rested, too, carrying my father to the workhouse.' The son rose, took the burden on his back again and turned with his wife for home. 'We'll manage somehow', he said.[4]

Here, then, is the vanguard and rearguard of the extended column of class in Edwardian Britain. There was much for future generations to demand. My theme in this chapter is the relation between the generations: and my focus is on the primordial link between them—the family. The nuclear family of parents and dependent children is the basic ascriptive unit of society. But it is much more. It is the reproductive social cell of class, of status, and of culture. If, therefore, we examine its history, we should see from another angle the continuities and changes of social structure in Britain in the period covered by our collective memory. We can map the journey of the advancing column. That we shall find significant differences in the substance and meaning of family life between now and three generations ago is already implicit in my account of the transformations of class, status, and party. The question now is how the pressures of these macroscopic social forces have modified the shape and process of the microcosm of their reproduction.

But before setting out to follow the trail of biological, social, and cultural reproduction, let us recognize the strange character of intellectual discussion of a subject so thoroughly known, so commonplace, so deeply and comprehensively learnt by everyone. The very word 'familiar' is used to denote what everybody knows. Can there then possibly be anything to add? I think so: and this is because we can have recourse to macroscopic information and to history—both necessary additions to the idiosyncratic experience on which personal knowledge is based.

I should also remark the passion that lies between personal knowledge and scholarship on the family—a vast literature of ideology. The family is both eulogized and vilified down the ages. Its immense power over the shaping of minds is constantly rediscovered. Confucius of the Analects tell us that: 'Those who in private life behave well towards their parents and elder brothers, in public life seldom show disposition to resist the authority of their superiors. And as for such men starting a revolution, no instance of it has ever occurred.'[5] Resentment of that power was vehemently expressed by Sir Edmund Leach in his Reith Lectures: 'Far from being the basis of the good society, the family with its narrow privacy and tawdry secrets, is the source of all discontents.'[6] There is no lack either of celebration of its beneficence. Here is Eleanor Rathbone in 1924:

Yet when we are considering society from any other point of view than the economic, we can all see well enough that, of all its institutions, the family is after all the institution that matters most. It is at once indispensable as a means to all the rest and, in a sense, an end in itself . . . the strongest emotions, the most enduring motives, the most universally accessible sources of happiness are concerned with this business of the family.[7]

So if we retreat awhile to the calmer and more arid regions of demography, it is to gain the light of factual perspective rather than to escape the heat of fierce engagement. Demographers have evolved the quaint custom of comparing fertility rates with the even quainter customs of the Hutterites—a flourishing community of agrarian fundamentalists in North Dakota. Demographers have chosen these people because they have the highest known levels of what is termed 'natural fertility', that is that fertility which is not affected by fertility-reducing social practices which are themselves dependent on the number of children already born. They have no deliberate birth control within marriage. On average, their families have over ten children. Against

the Hutterite yardstick, Britain and Europe have low repro-
ductivity. Even in the 1870s, before the onset of widespread
fertility control, Britain recorded little more than one-third
of the Hutterite rate. By 1931 fertility had plunged still
further by more than half of the 1871 level in England
and Wales, and slightly less than half in Scotland.[8]

This remarkable demographic transition is not peculiar
to Britain. British reproductive history is not specially
remarkable by comparison with other European countries,
except that it might have been expected that the first
industrial country would have been the first to experience
it, whereas in fact the transition came quite a lot later than
in France. It is also worth noting that, within Great Britain,
there has been more similarity of experience between regions, apart from Scotland, compared with the variability
within countries like Germany, Belgium, or Spain.

The demographic transition in Europe had three stages.
In the pre-industrial stage a slowly-growing population was
maintained by a balance of high death rates and high birth
rates. In the second stage of early industrialism extending
well into the nineteenth century, fertility habits remained
from the first stage, while a growing array of life-preserving
practices reduced mortality. Then in Stage III, fertility declined at a rate which overtook the still-falling mortality
rate until a new population equilibrium was reached by
a balance of low birth rates and low death rates.

This simplified description, leaving out migrations and
variations, though it roughly fits the facts and places our
period in Stage III, is useful more for the questions it raises
than for those it answers. Above all, it invites attention to
changes in the place of the family in society, both causal
and consequential, that have been involved. There is, however, at least one modification to the simple description
which must be added in order to bring experience since the
Second World War into view. There was a fertility upturn
after the War, followed by a downturn in the mid 1960s
which is still with us. I mention this later wobble in the
cycle to note the fact, rather than to promise that social
scientists have a precise theory to explain it.

The consequences of the Victorian population explosion are an important part of the social heritage of twentieth-century Britain. They include the growth of industrial cities at home,[9] and the global sweep of what might aptly be termed 'white peril' abroad, colonizing continents. Together foreign domination and domestic urbanization created an unprecedented empire within which the reminiscences of G. M. Young in Oxford and of the working man in Manchester combine to illustrate the comment that, if it was an empire on which the sun never set, there were parts of its heartland on which the sun never rose.

Figure 5.1.   United Kingdom Population 1901–1981

The birth rate, when our period opens, was still very high by today's European, if not by Hutterite, standards. In 1900 one-quarter of the married women were in childbirth every year. Yet thirty years later that proportion was down by one-half to one in eight. The earlier history of Stage III of the industrial demographic cycle need not concern us, though it continues to attract careful scholarship to its still unsolved problems.[10] One thing, however, is clear. For whatever reasons, the head of our metaphorical column had long since taken a decisive turn towards the ideal of the small family. And among the whys and hows of this movement towards what Young and Willmott now describe as the symmetrical family, there was a fall in infant mortality (Fig. 5.2), especially among professional and middle-class families, which set conditions for subsequent generations that have enabled us to think of the twentieth century as 'the century of the child'.

Figure 5.2. Infant Mortality 1900–1974 (Deaths under 1 year)

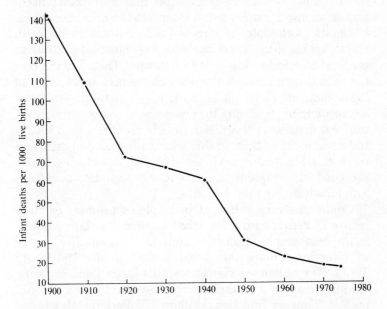

It may be, as Sir John Habakkuk has suggested, that it took time before people became fully aware of the implications of lower levels of mortality, that the middle classes did so first, and responded by planning and reducing their fertility within marriage. Working class men and women followed more slowly. When infant mortality had been high, it was both more difficult for married couples to predict the size of their surviving family, and less urgent for them to do so. And, incidentally, the luck of the draw under such conditions resulted in wider variations of family size than are common today.

Falling fertility during the first three decades of the century may be thought of, then, first as an adaptation to the continuing fall of infant mortality: people wanted, and were increasingly able, to control procreation according to their ideal size of family. But second, following the principle of stratified diffusion, we must notice that the course of reproduction in the twentieth century arrested the inverse relation of social class and fertility which had been inherited by Edwardian Britain. At that time, social distribution of the reproductive burden operated on the exact, if lunatic, principle of largest load on weakest back. In the following thirty years, the working class moved towards the earlier middle-class fertility norms. Those at the rear (or at any rate, towards the rear) of the historically marching column of social ranks, aspired to catch up with those ahead of them; and this they were able to do at roughly a ten-year distance. Class differences in fertility began slowly to be reduced: so that, in this sense, the stratified diffusion metaphor has to be modified—the tail was closing up on the head of the queue, the queue was beginning to reform into an advancing line abreast.

Could this very different principle of progress be fully realized? Perhaps not, for what I called the 'late wobble' in the demographic transition contained yet another change of direction among the social leaders in the 1940s and 1950s. They changed course towards larger families, while manual workers and their wives continued along the old path.[11] Thus we find Habakkuk in 1968 asking 'May it not be that the middle classes who in the 1870s led the country into the fashion of small families, are now leading us back to big families?'[12] He doubted whether the steps would be retraced very far, and the evidence of later years has justified his doubt, and there has been an important consequence. The fertility of those who have married since 1965, when projected to estimate completed family size, comes to just below 2.2 children for the average wife, which is just above the so-called 'replacement' figure of 2.1, and the completed family size of the lowest point of fertility reached by those who married around 1930. The demographic transition to an equilibrium of low fertility and low mortality may at last be complete.

There is now even the possible prospect of the elimination

or even the reversal of the inverse relation between class and fertility which began in the middle of the nineteenth century. There is, in other words, a possible future in which births are distrbuted between families in roughly the same way as income. Birth rates have become lowest in the middle of the class hierarchy. This pattern of U-shaped fertility by social class continues in the 1971 Census. The relevant data are shown in Table 5.1.

Table 5.1.[1]   Average family size for women married once only by social class of husband

| Marriage Duration | Social Class[2] of Husband | | | | | | |
	All	I	II	IIIA Non-manual	IIIB Manual	IV	V
10-14 years	2.24	2.23	2.12	1.99	2.28	2.30	2.56
15-19 years	2.29	2.25	2.17	2.00	2.34	2.37	2.66

Note 1:
I am indebted to my colleague, Michael Teitelbaum, for extracting this Table from the 1971 Census.

Note 2:
These are the Registrar General's classes. I is professional and managerial; II is intermediate; IIIA is routine white-collar; IIIB skilled manual; IV semi-skilled; and V unskilled.

Notice, however, that this is intended to show completed (or nearly completed) family size, and hence refers to women married in the 1950s. So it does not tell us what has been happening during the recent sharp fertility decline.

For this we need vital statistics for the past few years. These show that the overall number of legitimate births in England and Wales has declined by 24 per cent from 1970 to 1975 (in absolute terms the decline is from 720,000 to 549,000). But births to the top two social classes combined have declined very little (perhaps a few per cent), while those to the manual classes have declined by fully 30 per cent, and the III Non-manual Class decline is intermediate at 25 per cent. The proportion of all births to Social Classes I and II increased from 21 per cent in 1970 to 26 per cent in 1975, and the percentage born to the other social classes declined by lesser amounts (since they form the bulk of all births).

Hence the recent data are consistent with the postulated trend towards a further reduction in the gap between middle-class and working-class fertility. Whether this will result eventually in a direct positive relation between fertility and social class cannot be predicted, but the trends are at least consistent with such a development in the future. Nonetheless, the 1974 General Household Survey reported 'expected completed fertility of around 2.1 children for women married in 1965-9 to husbands in manual occupations, compared with 2.0 for those with husbands in non-manual occupations.'[13]

A summary of the transformation of family structure accompanying Stage III of the demographic transition is shown in Table 5.2.[14] The basic demographic development of the twentieth century is that the social classes have all adapted to a small family pattern. More people have gained greater freedom. Virtually all can now choose the timing of their parenthood. This is as important a feature of social change as any I could mention. And it has three further correlates, if not implications: the emancipation of women, the domestication of men, and the enrichment of childhood.

The place of women in society has been transformed. In his essay on *The Origin of the Family, Private Property, and the State*, Engels confuses class with status analysis, but arrests our attention, by declaring that 'the first class antagonism which appears in history coincides with the antagonism between men and women in monogamous marriage, and the first class oppression with that of the female sex by the male'.[15] No-one can read the history of marriage in our own time without being struck both by the material inequalities suffered by earlier generations of wives, and also by their reduction in more recent decades.

The burden of childbirth is central to the story. At the mid-point of the century, R. M. Titmuss summed it up by pointing out that, at the beginning of this century, a British woman aged 20 could expect to live 46 years longer. But approximately one-third of this life expectancy was to be

devoted to child-bearing and maternal care of infants.
Today a woman aged 20 can expect a further 55 years of
life. Of this longer expectation only about 7 per cent of the
years to be lived will be concerned with childbearing and
maternal care.[16]

Table 5.2. Some demographic changes over a century

Estimates of the average ages at certain vital events in England and Wales,
classified according to the year of birth of the persons to whom those events
occurred.

| | Year of birth | | | | | |
	1850	1870	1890	1910	1930	1950
1. First marriage						
Men	27	27	28	27	26	24
Women	26	26	26	25	24	22
2. Birth of first child						
Men	29	29	30	29	28	26
Women	28	28	28	27	26	24
3. Birth of last child						
Men	37	36	35	32	30	28
Women	36	35	33	30	28	26
4. Spouse's death						
Men	56	60	62	64	66	63
Women	55	58	61	63	65	67
5. Own death as widow or widower						
Men	75	77	79	80	81	82
Women	75	79	81	81	82	83

Source: See footnote 14.

But no less important than the virtual slavery of Edwardian working-class women on the wheel of childbearing was
the relation of women to the economy and the state. In
the earlier decades the great majority of families depended
entirely for their material support on male employment.
The establishment of a new position for the mother, independent of her link to the economy through her husband,
was therefore a prominent theme of feminist reform.
Eleanor Rathbone is again an outstanding voice. Child rearing, she argued, should be seen as a public service as well as
a private pleasure, and the costs spread accordingly. The
only practicable agent was the state, and Miss Rathbone

was, in effect, arguing for an extension of the social rights of citizenship for women. The main working-class demand in her day was for a 'living wage' for men. This she attacked as a continuation of ancient male tyranny. Even if achieved, the 'living wage' was intrinsically unrelated to family size. Women should not be regarded as dependants of the male in the labour market.

A wife and children and the wherewithall to keep them, are conceded to the wage earner as though they were part of the 'comforts and decencies promotive of better habits' for which he may reasonably ask . . . But if he prefers to use the margin thus allowed him for breeding pigeons or racing dogs, or for some other form of personal gratification, instead of for keeping a family, that is assumed to be his affair, not the State's or his employer's.[17]

In the event, the State response was less than fulsome and the political descendents of Eleanor Rathbone, like Margaret Wynn,[18] or Frank Field,[19] still vigorously point out that both social security and taxation policies continue to treat families less favourably than bachelors, spinsters, and childless couples.

The State has contributed indirectly towards the liberation of women, especially through the expansion of health services and education. But the loneliness of mothers with young children is still well attested and the absence of communal provision for such women remains an unsatisfied need. Meanwhile, more direct emancipating influences have come from developed methods of birth control and, most important, the gradual movement of women, including married women, into employment. In the first two decades of this century less than 10 per cent of married women in Britain went out to work: in 1951 the percentage was 21.74: by 1966 it had risen to 38.08,[20] and by 1976 to 49.[21] The slow spread of affluence has also played its part in combination with the invention of power appliances to relieve some of the drudgery of housework. Suburbanization and geographical mobility have provided escape for some from the matrilocal matriarchies of the traditional urban working-class communities—a point which reminds us that women's liberation has discriminated so far in favour of younger as against older women. So we could go on through a catalogue of economic and technical changes, and their consequences, which have made possible the trend towards *The Symmetrical Family* of Young and Wilmott.

The correlative history, which is rather less noticed, is that of husbands and fathers. This too is a social transformation deserving its own detailed history. It would begin with young men of the Victorian upper-middle classes moving into marriage with prejudices mitigated at least to the point of co-operating in planned parenthood. Stratified diffusion would again emerge. Later, working men returning from the First World War had to accommodate, in many cases, to wives who had acquired a more independent outlook from having worked in the munitions factories, and from having run their homes unaided. Literacy and the wireless pushed back horizons between the Wars. Unlike previous wars, the Second World War did not tip the demographic balance in favour of men by killing more men than women: the number of men and women remained roughly in balance, the reserve army of women disappeared.

Still more important, seventy years ago, working men typically lived in local occupationally homogeneous communities, of which mining and dock work were the classic examples.[22] Such communities evolved essentially male public organizations—the pub, the betting shop, the football club; organizations which loosened marriage bonds and took resources away from women and children. But the newer patterns of inter-war industry around London and Birmingham, in the Home Counties and the Midlands, took their toll of the older male domination—reducing class solidarity perhaps and inviting more romantic love certainly. Particularly after the Second World War, hours of work were reduced, holidays lengthened, home ownership became more common, children were less ever-present, and men were drawn into a more intimate and longer spousehood than their predecessors had ever known. We noted in Chapter 2 that privatization was a key description of the affluent worker in Luton by the 1960s.[23] It involved a closer, more co-operative, domesticity for millions of men.

Perhaps the growth of the pornographic industry and the verbal obscenities which are hurled across football stands are each in their way further correlates of the pressure on men to adopt the new familial civilities.

Nevertheless, the story should not be exaggerated. The journey to a symmetrical family, with full psychic and material equality for women, is far from completed. Nor is it the only possible end to the journey. Looking back we can say that the social column has advanced and that the working-class is much less conspicuously relegated to its rearguard. Yet the new freedom is by no means costless. Divorce and separation have largely replaced death as disruptors of the early and middle years of marriage. In 1974 there were well over three-quarters of a million people who had been divorced and had not re-married. We cannot, of course, weigh the cost or gauge the misery caused by marital breakdown now or at any point in the past. We can estimate roughly that one-quarter of contemporary marriages will go through some kind of breakdown. We can also agree with Young and Willmott that their symmetrical family, since it asks more of its partners, exposes them also to greater strain and higher risk of failure. Moreover, as Juliet Cheetham has put it:

> the possibility of controlling fertility, although usually accepted as an unqualified blessing, brings its own problems. It challenges women to contemplate social roles other than full-time motherhood. Acceptance of this challenge threatens prevailing assumptions about family life and about equality. Efforts to maintain the status quo frustrate women's aspirations and achievements. Discontent and conflict may be necessary preliminaries to human advancement but they are not comfortable to live with.[24]

As the Finer Report on one-parent families shows, the woman left to raise children alone is among the most pathetic casualties of an affluent society.[25]

Nonetheless, the third estate of the nuclear family—the child—has been the chief beneficiary of the developments I have sketched. If I have to choose a single word to identify the changes in social reproduction in this century it would be 'individualism'. This is the motif that has increasingly informed every aspect of child rearing, whether in the family or in the public sphere of playgroups, clubs, schools, holiday camps, juvenile courts, or borstals. The essential background, of course, is the decline of infant mortality and the spread of the small family. Yet this move to smaller families, though important in itself, has to be seen as the base and not the whole edifice of a more general trend towards higher standards of upbringing. For example, of those children born in the decade around the First World War only one-fifth grew up in owner-occupied houses, though in families with, on average, 3.4 children. Those born in the decade after the Second World War belonged to families with on average 2.1 children, and well over one-third of them were owner-occupiers.[26] Most children in the early years of the century grew up in the streets of industrial cities, while there has been a more recent move to the suburbs in council estates and private dwellings. A working-class area is not now, so much as it once was, a kind of dormitory annex to the work place. The working-class family has become less closely geared to the factory hooter. This, combined with shorter hours of work, may well have increased the amount of attention men give to their children. On the other hand, the gradual growth of women's employment outside the home may have had an opposite effect on mother-child relations.

Children now are more likely to come from middle-class families. The working class has fallen and the middle classes have risen as suppliers of children. Before the First World War more than two-thirds were of working-class origin. Moreover, even within the working class, the chances of being born into the home of a skilled rather than an unskilled worker, and into a smaller rather than a larger family, with rather higher income and rather better housing, gradually improved for those born later in the century. The norm shifted, in other words, from the description given by Richard Hoggart[27] of his childhood in Hunslet in the 1920s to the modest prosperity enjoyed by Britain since the 1950s.

With these changes in material conditions, there has been

a transformation of relations with parents, especially mothers. There has been, so to say, a Freudian revolution. For those born, like me, in the 1920s, it was as if their mothers had read and inwardly digested James Thurber's book *Let Your Mind Alone*. Those born after the War had mothers who, through women's magazines and the mass media, have absorbed some version or other of the psycho-analytic approach to children, heavily slanted in the direction of hedonism.[28]

But though the standards and expectations of childhood have undoubtedly risen in the lifetime of the oldest Britons now alive, we must not forget that throughout our period the probability of membership of a large family, and of low income, poor housing, illness, and early death, had continued to mark off the social classes from each other. Some children have continued to grow up in traditional working-class communities in the industrial cities, and a deprived minority among the working class is variously estimated at about half-a-million, even today. In December 1975 there were 380,000 families with children who were normally on supplementary benefit. The number of children involved was 810,000. Poverty in large families remains a hazard of childhood.[29] For example, though the average size of completed family among manual workers has fallen, a description of the childhood circumstances of those living in the Birmingham educational priority area in 1969 showed that no less than 91 per cent came from families of three or more children.[30]

What, then, are we to say about relations between the generations? From one point of view, the changes I have traced in the twentieth century seem to have created a children's paradise. No age has ever been more child-centred, or gone so far towards making death socially invisible. Yet parental anxiety, exacerbated by marital uncertainty, is endemic. Fathers, and more especially mothers, inhabit a world which takes away their control over, and simultaneously insists on the responsibility for, the fate of their children. Most parents have lived through a dramatic shift in the standards expected of them. It is not enough, as it once was, to look after bodily health and physical security. Parents must also answer for the mental and moral character of their sons and daughters, despite influences from the street, the so-called peer group, the mass media and youth culture which children cannot escape, and with which parents cannot contend. They are increasingly made to feel amateurs in a difficult professional world. The old 'Us and Them' of the working-class mother is now a more generalized division between the inner life of families of all classes, and the external public forces. Such circumstances, together with the appreciation of schooling as a matter largely beyond family control, which determines the future jobs and incomes of their children, may add up to intense frustration. Relations between the generations in all classes are prone to anxiety and conflict, and the family is hard-pressed.

This is strange when we consider how much the twentieth century deserves its description as the 'century of the child'. So much of modern politics has been about children. Not only increasing educational expenditure but also infant and maternity services, population policies, family allowances, adoption and fostering, treatment of young offenders, and so on. Even the principal objective all over the world of economic growth is essentially justified as 'for the children'. The old are relatively political outcasts. The future is all. 'Trailing clouds of glory do they come.' We have lived through a revolution, demographic, economic, and social, as a result of which the child has become the quality product of industrial society. The recalcitrant Andy Capp who says, 'What have my grandchildren done for me that I should care for them?' is at best a pre-freudian anachronism.

We should start by recognizing the frustration of the modern parent—whether a West Indian mother in Brixton who is baffled by the apparent failure of the school to teach her boy either good letters or good manners, or the anxious suburban father calculating the costs and benefits of buying a place for his boy in the private sector now that the comprehensive school is the only alternative.

It is said in educational circles that the monitoring role of Her Majesty's inspectors has been lost in recent years and, if this is so, it is partly because they have lost confidence as to what schools ought to be doing and therefore the authority to guide those they inspect. They deserve sympathy, for the loss of confidence is not only theirs. We *all* live in confusion as to what is the good life. Rereading Richard Hoggart's account of working-class life before the 1950s, I am struck by the integration of ordinary families in those days with the moral traditions of the old class and Christian society which he so accurately and lovingly described. That moral structure has ebbed away fast under the assault of the classless inequalities and the secular materialism of the post-war world and, in the process, the familial controls over upbringing have steadily attenuated.

A traditional culture weakened by multiple forces of change falters in its transmission to the next generation and the lonely crowd of adolescent age-mates look to each other for guidance. They too, like their parents, are essentially powerless, for all their newly-found access to relative material prosperity. Their powerlessness is reflected in their collective amnesia, their unknowingness of the history of their conditions, and even more in their uncertainty as to their future. No wonder that fashionability, hedonism, and a desparate individualism serve as substitutes for a securely-held morality. Hoggart's working-class family is romantically remote now.

Of course, they were never church or chapel attenders in substantial proportions but, as Hoggart put it:

They believe, first, in the purposiveness of life. Life has a meaning, must have a meaning. One does not bother much about defining it, or pursue abstract questions as to its nature or the implications which follow from such a conclusion: 'We're 'ere for a purpose', they say, or 'There must be some purpose or we wouldn't be 'ere.' And that there is a purpose presupposes that there must be a God. They hold to what G. K. Chesterton called 'the dumb certainties of existence', and Reinhold Niebuhr, 'primary religion'. Equally simply, they hold to what George Orwell called 'those things (like free-will and the existence of the individual) which we know to be so, though all the arguments are against them'.[31]

Since Hoggart wrote not only the further decline of church and chapel, but also the changes in the typical position of married women—their reduced fertility and their sharply increased rate of paid employment—have been of greater moment in changing the character of the learning process among children than all the expansion and reorganization of schools which has gone on since the Education Act of 1944, including its development of schooling, its provision of secondary education for all, and its raising of the school leaving age.

In short, a weakening of the bond between parent and child, and exacerbation of conflict between them, are a fundamental and paradoxical part of the so-called century of the child. From one point of view this may be seen in the growing power of public authorities to override the traditional rights of parents over children, albeit justified in the name of ever-rising standards of child care. Standards belong to experts. From another point of view, weakening bonds and sharpened conflicts are seen in child-avoidance by adults. This was, of course, always the way of the rich down the ages through such bodies as house-slaves, tutors, and (in this context aptly named) public schools. Characteristically, it now takes the form, in middle-class districts, of an endless round of parties and play activities which in effect share out the stint of child-minding on an informal rota system, releasing the other mothers. In the working class, as Brian Jackson keeps reminding us, the child-minding industry has become an essential adjunct of recognized women's employment, punitively contained by a public administration in the vain hope that it will some-how go away. From another point of view, the parent and the teacher tacitly conspire to retreat from the harsh realities of their own lack of confidence to leave the children corralled before the television set. Later, adolescents are given up to their peer-group activities in segregated terri-tories which they increasingly monopolize, such as the disco, the football terrace, the student union, and the pop music festival. These age-segregated phenomena are surely among those which the Martian anthropologist would pick out as significant features of a modern urban upbringing.

Meanwhile, the impact of class on upbringing may have been changing with respect to the nature of transmitted capital. In a pure class society it is, or was, material capital which differentiated the classes, and education basically served to put a stamp of class culture on fates already decided by class origin. The social reproduction of generations was primarily a transmission of material capital and therefore of its attendant inequality of income and opportunity.

But as the economy slowly developed its technology, and gradually complicated its division of labour, the fate of a family's children began to turn more on the successful transmission of cultural rather than material capital. Both still exist, of course, and are partially interchangeable—for example, conspicuously in a private or marketed system of schools. But cultural capital is of increasing importance. It is affirmed and publicly recognized in degrees, certificates, and credentials. And it is acquired first and foremost through familial transmission—for example, through knowledge of how to use the public properties of libraries and museums, through elaborated language codes which are indispensable to success at school, through appropriate levels of academic aspiration reinforced in the home, through information about learning or job opportunities.

The result is (just as much in Communist Russia or Capitalist America as in Britain) that the social reproduction of generations is a reproduction of a hierarchy of cultural capital. This permits considerable mobility for a minority upwards and downwards in the hierarchy, but its main feature remains the continuity of familial status between generations.

6 Mobility and education

To draw a complete picture of social and cultural reproduction we must take account not only of the family but of all the institutions which pass on skills, knowledge, and belief through channels other than those of genetic transmission. The development of education as an active agent of cultural evolution and social selection is one of the more obvious features of change in British society in the twentieth century.

I want, in this chapter, to ask about educational change by putting one version of a central question about any society: is it an open one? And I choose this approach because 'the open society' has been the traditional aim of liberal policy, with education in the forefront as one of its principal means.

The question can, of course, have many meanings. For the liberal it may turn on whether there is access to knowledge and freedom to use it. The interest of the egalitarian is different. He is typically concerned to question unequal distributions of skill and knowledge and to assume that, unless there is proof to the contrary, inequality of outcome in the social distribution of knowledge is a measure of *de facto* inequality of access. The ensuing debate has provided the stuff of educational politics in Britain, as in other countries in this century. Behind it lies the more general question of what distributions between the members of each new generation are possible and desirable.

The study of mobility can throw empirical light on these questions. I shall therefore take advantage of the findings which have been emerging from the Oxford mobility study to which I referred in Chapter 3. The basic material consists of skeletal life histories—familial, educational, and occupational— of a national sample of 10,000 men aged 20-64 in England and Wales in 1972. Innumerable questions from innumerable theories can be asked of such a body of data. The central intention was to ask questions about mobility. The idea of mobility implies movement from somewhere to somewhere else and the 'somewhere' in question may in principle be any social or geographical position. In the sociological literature it usually means some kind of class, status, prestige, or socio-economic position.

Has post-war reform equalized opportunity? What happens to those who are born into different circumstances of power and advantage? These are some of the traditional questions in the long history of British 'political arithmetic'. In 1949 Professor Glass and his colleagues at the London School of Economics pioneered a study of mobility in that tradition.[1] Twenty years later my colleagues and I at Nuffield College, Oxford, judged that, after an intervening generation of social democratic reform, it was time to look again.

However, this is by no means the only approach to the complicated question of social mobility. Another, followed by John Goldthorpe, pursues an interest in the processes of class formation.[2] A third, which we glimpsed in Chapter 4, examines the correlates and consequences of mobility in electoral choice.[3] But whatever the approach we do well to appreciate the complexity of movements between social positions to which I pointed in Chapter 3. The intricacy of the structure of class, status, and party in Britain has already emerged in previous chapters. None of these dimensions, separately or together, yield a unitary hierarchy. Nor is the passage of individuals through the social structure a simple repetition of the experiences of one generation by the next. As we have seen, there have been fluctuations and trends in births and deaths, and in the occupational and other social positions to be filled. Moreover, mobility can be thought of as either group or individual, and either between or within generations.

With these various meanings and methodological cautions in mind we can begin to analyse the fluidity of the society experienced by recent generations in Britain. We can again use the simplification of three social strata of social classes, ignoring or evading the many sociologically created conceptual traps which are found in the study of social stratification, for example the vulgar Marxist theology of two classes at war in capitalist society, or the vulgar liberal conception of a continuous hierarchy of prestige or status which would make every man a class.

The first of our three strata can be taken, as before, to mean the *middle class*: professional, managerial, and administrative occupational groups and higher technicians and their wives and children. Taken by their *origin* (that is, classified by their fathers' occupation when they were 14 years old) these formed 13.3 per cent of men in England and Wales in 1972. The second stratum is a heterogeneous *lower-middle class* of non-manual employees, small proprietors, self-employed artisans, but also lower-grade technicians and supervisors of manual workers. They made up 30.8 per cent of the 1972 men by origin. The third stratum is the *working class*—industrial manual workers and agricultural workers whether skilled, semi-skilled, or unskilled. They made up the other 55.9 per cent by origin.

In this simple classification each individual has one of three classes as an origin, but also (judged by his own job ten years after entering the labour market) one of the same three as a destination.[4] Distributed by destination as distinct from where they had started as boys, they appear in the following array:

	Social Class Destinations Percentage
Middle class	20.1
Lower-middle class	24.9
Working class	55.0

It is immediately apparent that the structure of origins is different from that of destinations for this generation of Britons. On balance there has been movement out of the working class and lower-middle class into the middle class. We will return to this question of trends. But for the time being let us stick to our snapshot survey and put the origins and destinations together to form the following grid of inter-generational class mobility (Table 6.1).

Table 6.1. Inter-generational class mobility: adult males, England and Wales, 1972

| Origins | Destinations (Ten years after entry to work) | | |
	Middle class %	Lower Middle %	Working class %
Middle class	7.0	3.7	2.6
Lower Middle	7.0	9.9	13.9
Working class	6.1	11.3	38.5
			100

We now see nine kinds of inter-generational experience, each one measured as a percentage of the total. The columns of the grid tell us about *inflow* between generations to the three *destination* classes. The rows show *outflow* from *origin* classes. The diagonal cells from top left to bottom right denote those who were found, ten years after starting their working lives, in the social class where they started. The cells below and to the left of the diagonal are occupied by those who would be correctly described as having had upward mobility if our three social classes were arranged in a strict hierarchy. The cells to the right and above the diagonal would be men who have been downwardly mobile.

We should again remind ourselves at this point that this is a simplified picture. It conflates the experience of successive cohorts of births and entry into the labour market, it ignores the heterogeneity of the three social classes, and it obscures intra-generational movement. Thus, for example, John Goldthorpe and Catriona Llewellyn, examining more closely the experience of those who had been born into, and were also found as adults in the middle classes in 1972, show that half of them did *not* start their working lives in this social class, but began in a lower non-manual or manual job and later moved to a middle-class job.[5] In other words, our patterns and proportions of inter-generational stability of the middle class disguise intra-generational instability, what these researchers call 'counter-mobility'.

Nevertheless, returning to the simpler inter-generational picture, we can say that the typical Englishman or Welshman was born into and stayed in the working class. This is the largest group, more than three times as big as the next largest, which is those who started in lower-middle class families and became manual workers. The three smallest groups are all mobile ones—from working class to middle class (6.1 per cent), from middle class to lower-middle class (3.7 per cent), and from middle class to working class (2.6 per cent).

Is this an open society? Certainly it is not a caste society. If we add all three diagonal cells, it turns out that the proportion who stay as adults in the social class in which they spent their childhood is little more than half (55.4 per cent). A very substantial minority of Englishmen and Welshmen in the last generation have been socially mobile (44.6 per cent). If we look at the rows (outflow) it turns out that, while 7 per cent were born into the middle class and stayed there, 3.7 per cent went to the lower middle class and 2.6 per cent went to the working class, together accounting for the 13.3 per cent of middle-class origin. If we look at the columns (inflow) it further becomes clear that the idea, which is quite widespread among sociologists, that the élite have effective means of closing their ranks against the entry of other men's children is clearly a false one if by élite we mean what we have here defined as the middle class. The number of newcomers from other social classes is getting on for twice the number of those who are, so to speak, middle-class by birth. This is a similar picture to that presented by Geoff Payne for Scotland.[6] The number of middle-class sons who moved into the lower-middle or the working class is not very far short of those who stayed where they were born.

Thus if we look at our three social classes expecting

to find closed hereditary groups then the middle class
disappoints us. Indeed it is the working class which approxi-
mates more to this notion. The typical factory worker is at
least a second generation proletarian, while the middle-class
man who looks at his fellows will find that nearly two out
of every three of them have come from birth in another
social class. The first industrial nation now combines a
mature working class with an *arriviste* middle class.

So far we have examined outflow and inflow as they
have occurred and in relation to each other. An alternative
is to consider them in relation to an external criterion. Politically this may be conceived as the open society. Statisti-
cally, in the way which the London School of Economics
1949 study made standard for subsequent mobility research,
the same notion may be represented as that of 'perfect
mobility', that is what the numbers or percentages would
have been if destinations were randomly related to origins.
The point is to compare actual movement with a defined
hypothetical pattern of movement. Essentially the same
method is to compare the *relative* chances of moving from
given origins to given destinations. For example, the chances
of becoming middle-class are highest for middle-class sons,
more than half of whom retained their position, while
fewer than one in nine working-class sons moved into the
middle class. Notice too that the chances of moving out
from the working class were less than one in three, while
the chances of moving out from a middle-class childhood
were very nearly one to one. Another and summary way of
answering the 'open society' question is to measure the
strength of the bond between fathers and son. In a fully
open society the correlation between the social class of
fathers and sons would be 0.0 and in a rigid caste society it
would be 1.0 In fact, calculated on our 1972 data, the correlation between father's occupation and son's occupation
in 1972 is about 0.36.[7]

The search for an explanation of these patterns of mobility naturally leads us to schools and credentials. Table 6.2
summarizes the educational career of each of the nine
groups we have distinguished. It amalgamates the experience

of those who had passed, at various times, through the expanding system of schooling in England and Wales from before the First to after the Second World War.

Table 6.2. Education and mobility

	Private Primary Schooling %	Selective Secondary Schooling %	School Exams. %	Some F.E. Qualifications %	Univ. Degree %
1. Stable middle class	32.0	88.4	82.0	33.1	29.8
2. Middle	24.9	65.1	53.6	17.2	5.7
3. Middle to working	3.8	33.5	15.1	7.0	0.5
4. Lower-middle to working	11.7	67.9	62.1	34.1	13.5
5. Stable lower-middle	7.5	44.3	27.1	5.6	1.0
6. Lower-middle to working	3.0	21.9	8.1	1.8	0.1
7. Working to middle	1.6	63.1	58.5	32.3	12.8
8. Working to lower-middle	2.0	32.2	20.2	3.9	1.1
9. Stable working	0.6	14.7	4.6	0.4	0.1
ALL	5.8	34.8	23.9	10.3	4.3

So far, incidentally, we have avoided using the language of upward and downward mobility out of respect for the fact that our three social classes must not be thought of as discretely arranged in a hierarchy. When occupations are scaled in terms of what Goldthorpe and Hope call 'general desirability',[8] as judged by the population at large, the resulting rank order or scale values only roughly correspond to groupings which might be held to form classes through similarity of market and work position. In the case of the three social classes we are using here the middle-class occupations hardly overlap at all with those of the other two. But there is considerable overlap between the lower-middle and the working class and, of course, considerable heterogeneity within them as to judgements of their 'general desirability'. With this general caution in mind, however, we may for the sake of convenience use the metaphor of upward and downward movement.

The educational profiles of our nine mobility categories, apart from yielding recognizable stereotypes of Britons, show a regular patterning of the relations between education and mobility. It can be seen from the underlined rows of Table 6.2 that the educational norms for each of the three social classes, as represented by those who have had stable membership, are positively related to social class both of origin and destination. Thus the stable middle-class men are composed of 88 per cent with selective secondary schooling, and 30 per cent with a university education, compared with 44 per cent and 1 per cent for the stable lower-middle class, and 15.0 per cent and 0.1 per cent for the stable working class. In other words, those who find jobs in the higher occupational categories have more education and more qualifications. This will surprise no-one.

Looking at the other six categories of those who have moved from their birth position, it is equally clear that mobility involves realignment of social class membership according to educational qualifications. Thus, those who have moved upwards have, in the process, exceeded the educational norms of their origin group, and 'those who have moved downwards have had less educational advantage and attained fewer education qualifications. This pattern is absolutely regular. But there are some details worth remarking. If we look at the destination classes it appears that those who move up from below do not, on average, have as much educational qualification as those who have been stable in the destination class in question. Similarly, those who move down still have a rather higher educational profile than the stable members of the class they join and, which follows from our remarks on the upwardly mobile, a still higher one than those who have joined the same destination class from below.

Putting these two tendencies together, that is, the association of education with social origin and also its association with mobility, what we then find is that exchange between the social classes is also a partial exchange of the educationally qualified. For example, those who have moved from the middle class to the working class include only 1 per cent of graduates, while those who have moved from the working class to the middle class include 13 per cent of graduates. There is thus, in the process of mobility, exchange not only of individuals but of social investment of education and qualifications which maintains a differential distribution of social qualities between the social classes. I would lay particular emphasis on this aspect of the reproduction of the stratification system. Inter-generational mobility serves to reconstitute the general pattern of distribution of attributes of the different social classes.

At the same time this evidence on education and mobility in Britain shows that neither a division into social classes nor into mobility groups completely differentiates the population by their education. It is just as important to notice that the great majority of those born into the middle class did *not* go to private primary schools or to universities as it is to notice that those who were either born into, or made their way into, the middle class were more likely to have had these educational experiences than those who came from, or went to, either the lower-middle or the working class.

Now, we may ask, what are the trends in mobility? In terms of our metaphor, this means turning a snapshot into a film. The method in one form or another is that of cohort analysis. But there are many dangers here. The birth cohorts of our sample are not strict random samples of birth cohorts in the history which they are made to represent, if only because while all sons have one and only one father, the converse is far from true. Moreover, it is difficult to know how far differences between birth cohorts are attributable to age or to the particular period of history in which a cohort reaches a given age. Given the background of change in the occupational structure which we have already discussed in Chapter 2, there is every reason to be cautious in interpreting trends from a survey of the kind on which we are relying here.

Nevertheless, bearing in mind all these qualifications, I cannot do better than to paraphrase the most recent findings from the Oxford mobility study on 'Trends in Class Mobility' by J. H. Goldthorpe, Clive Payne, and Catriona Llewellyn.[9] These authors show, most adroitly, that the view one can take of the question as to whether Britain has become a more open society will depend crucially on the method of measurement. They use three methods. First, following the method we have used in Table 6.2, they gauge 'absolute mobility rates' by tabulating the percentage movement from origins to destinations (which may be transit points in the case of first jobs or jobs ten years after entry to the labour market, and in any case cannot be taken as a pure definition of 'occupational maturity') in defined classes or occupational groups. On this measure they conclude that there has been a trend towards greater openness in that the younger men in the sample had better chances than older men of similar origins, of being found in the higher class positions, that is, in professional, higher technical, administrative, or managerial jobs.

Then, second, these authors turn to a simple measure of 'relative mobility rates', using disparity ratios. Absolute rates are those which are more or less visible to the participants (social actors) themselves. Relative rates are sociologists' concepts and not necessarily part of the social consciousness of participants: they relate the chances of mobility of men in different classes to some statistically-defined norm or model, such as that of random relation between fathers' and sons' class position to which I have referred as perfect mobility. Measurement of relative rates of mobility by disparity ratios is a method which allows for change in the structure of classes or occupations. It enables us to gauge changes in the chances of being found in given destinations among men of differing origins. The disparity ratios are ratios between outflow percentages. For example, in a society divided into two classes the proportion of sons of Class I who themselves held Class I jobs as a proportion of all Class I sons is expressed as a ratio of the proportion of Class II sons who gained Class I jobs from the total number of Class II sons. Put formally, the disparity ratios would be

$$\frac{f_{11}}{f_1} \Bigg/ \frac{f_{21}}{f_2} \quad \text{and} \quad \frac{f_{22}}{f_2} \Bigg/ \frac{f_{12}}{f_1}$$

On this measure, the authors conclude that stability rather than change is the outstanding feature of inter-generational class mobility in Britain in recent decades. Whereas absolute rates give an impression of trends towards greater openness in the sense of there being increasing rates of upward movement into the expanding higher levels of the class structure, the relative rates show that these expanding opportunities have been fairly equally shared out between men of different class origins so as to produce no change in their relative chances of access. In the recent period, moreover, while the working class has been shrinking, the relative as well as the absolute chances of men of middle-class origin being found in manual work have also declined. In short, relative class chances have been stable or increasingly unequal.

Then, third, the authors use a more complex measure of relative rates by the use of odds ratios defined formally in a 2×2 mobility table as:

$$\frac{f_{21}/f_{22}}{f_{11}/f_{22}}$$

That is, measuring whether the relative chances of the son of a Class I father being himself found in Class I rather than Class II are changing over time at the same rate as the relative chances of the sons of a Class II father being found in Class I rather than Class II. On this approach the conclusion

is again reached that there have been no systematic or
general shifts in relative mobility. The relative chances of
men from two different classes of origin being found in
one rather than another of two different class destinations
have not changed.

In short, in a period in which the occupational division
of labour in Britain was transformed to offer more middle-
class opportunities, there was continuity in the underlying
processes of inter-generational class mobility. Moreover,
though there may have been some specific trands in relative
chances of movement between particular classes, the evidence is that increased fluidity is to be found only when
the class position of sons and their fathers are compared at
a relatively early stage in the working life of the son. When
inter-generational mobility is measured using class origin
and the point of 'occupational maturity' (beyond which
there is little likelihood of further major shifts in class
position), such trends as are to be found are in the direction
of reduced social fluidity. In general, however, a model of
'constant social fluidity' best fits the data.

If these are the mobility patterns and their educational
correlates, how are we to explain them in relation to familial and educational development? My account of social
reproduction in Chapter 5 was a description of the supply
of children. But the supply of children in turn constitutes
a demand for education which, though fashioned by the
principle of stratified diffusion, and made to fluctuate
quantitatively by changes in the birth rate, has risen quali-
tatively throughout the century. The demand has been met
by a state policy of educational expansion. And this policy,
advocated originally by Victorian liberal optimists, has
always been seen as the promise of new and higher levels
of both material prosperity and elevated culture for the
nation, happily accompanied by more equality, since to
raise the supply of educated labour would result in a reduction of its relative price.

Our studies in Oxford enable us now to assess the extent
to which the Victorian vision has been realized. That assessment has to be less than the hopes of the reformers, though

I should immediately add that it also contains no support for those 'Black Paper' writers who would have us believe that educational standards have declined. Expansion there has been, and with it a cumulation of cultural capital. The outstanding feature of the state selective secondary schools, which developed after the 1902 Education Act, was always that the majority of their pupils were 'first generation' recruits to advanced education.

Nevertheless, we have been forced to the depressing conclusion that over the century so far, the unequal relative educational chances of boys from different class origins have been remarkably stable, and that the conventional picture of a steady trend towards equality has been an optimistic myth. The metaphor of the column with which we began in Chapter 5 does, apparently, work for education if not for fertility.

What, then, is the connection between school and work? Launching a 'great education debate' in 1976, the Prime Minister, James Callaghan, called for a closer link between education and the needs of industry. This is an old story, which is not to say it is untrue. Every single generation in the history of Britain as an industrial nation has been told that the schools are failing to provide the skills of workers, managers, and professionals needed by a modernizing economy. This was the case when Britain led the world in the rate of economic growth just as much as it is the case now when it is portrayed as the ailing Western country, the sick man of Europe, the ageing bankrupt, etc. That, of course, is another story, which could be quite differently, if debatably, presented as one of a country with a deep and lively tradition of democracy and one which is leading the world rather than trailing behind it in pursuing the application of democratic principles beyond the polling booth in the factory and work place, the home, and the school.

Mr. Callaghan is entirely right if he means that there is a rather tenuous connection between educational and occupational changes in modern Britain. Both the output of qualified people from the educational system and the intake of professional, managerial, and white-collar manpower into the work force have risen year by year, especially in recent decades. But there is no automatic supply/demand relation between the two upward movements. They have proceeded independently of each other and no simple conclusion can be drawn along the lines of praising or blaming the schools for the level of efficiency or national income or unemployment or any other aspect of the economy. Of course, for an individual, job choice and protection against unemployment are improved the longer he stays in school and the more he collects educational certificates. But the wealth of the nation, the range of occupational opportunities, and the level of employment for British society as a whole are determined by quite other forces, such as the amount of investment, the international market, and the collective attitudes towards work and leisure which prevail at any given time. Education alone cannot create either wealth or welfare.

That truth exposes the limitation of Mr. Callaghan's invitation to debate. The underlying issue is the social reproduction of generations. In another phrase, it is about social engineering. One of the irritating features of the 'Black Paper' ideology put out by Mr. Rhodes Boyson, Professor Cox, the Institute of Economic Affairs, and other conservatives, is that they say radicals believe in using the schools for social engineering while they want to get back to education. This is a verbal trick. It illicitly suggests that there is a choice, which there is not. The reproduction of a generation is *always* social engineering. The issue is engineering for what? For egalitarians, it is to make a reality of democratic values. For the 'Black Paper' writers, it is social engineering for a society of market liberalism and hierarchy. We should argue these ends and not pretend that the egalitarians are somehow and sinfully introducing corrupting politics into the purity of learning.

The Oxford mobility study enables us to trace the educational experience of boys in four successive decennial birth cohorts—1913-22, 1923-32, 1933-42, and 1943-52.[10] From the beginning of the century until the 1960s the crucial point of educational selection was at 11 plus. At this age all children took tests of intelligence and attainment. From this result the most fateful decision was whether children went to a grammar or technical school, or to an unselected elementary or (after 1944) secondary modern school. The proportion of children attending grammar schools increased in every decade. Even for those born between 1943 and 1952 the supply of grammar school places kept pace with the growth in total population, although not with the growth in the middle classes. The proportion of grammar school children from all classes went on increasing right up to the mid-point of the century, the relative rates being highest for the working class, but the absolute increases being highest for the middle class. Then for the first post-war generation, the working class managed to protect its gains, while the now expanded middle classes lost some of theirs, though without falling back to the position they held a generation earlier. Hence, with respect to the grammar school, there were increased chances in general throughout the period and some narrowing of class differentials, both relative to the average, and relative to each other. The technical school picture, however, is very different. After the 1944 Education Act these schools began to disappear. The expansion of the grammar schools in the post-war period and before the comprehensive movement got underway in the 1960s was largely at the expense of the technical schools. What the working class gained through the expansion of the grammar schools, they largely lost through the decline of the technical schools. Thus, comparing the 1913-22 with the 1943-52 birth cohort, one hundred working-class families sent an extra eight boys to grammar school, but they also sent eight fewer to technical schools.

Meanwhile, after the 1944 Act, the emphasis of expansion gradually shifted to the later stages of secondary schooling, and to post-secondary provision. Here the class-differentiating forces continued to operate. The rewards for success and survival were high, and the result was that the amount spent on the education of children of different origin, far from equalizing chances, helped to maintain class inequality. Over the period as a whole, those born into professional and managerial families had three times as much spent on them as those born into the families of agricultural labourers. Those who went to selective secondary schools, private schools, and on to post-secondary education, especially in universities, were also relatively more expensively raised. The upshot was, as I pointed out in Chapter 2, that although there was a slight tendency to greater equality of investment in the school education of boys from different classes, the development of post-secondary education more than counterbalanced this equalizing effect because it was disproportionaly used by boys from the middle class.

We can illustrate these processes in twentieth-century Britain by focusing on the university graduate. The rise of the graduate in the twentieth century has occasionally been compared with that of the gentry in an earlier age and is sometimes described as a new estate (Eric Ashby[11]), an educational class (Ralph Dahrendorf[12]), or as the central element in the techno-structure of modern society (J. K. Galbraith[13]). These conceptions may be put into perspective by looking at the numbers revealed in the national sample of men aged 20–64 in England and Wales in 1972. It is not, of course, the whole picture, nor one from the main angle of vision of the research which is intended to portray the degree of openness or fluidity in modern British occupational and social structure. We can ask four simple questions:

1. How many men had university compared with other possible kinds of education? This is Table 6.3.
2. How much has the graduate element increased over the course of the century? This is Table 6.4.
3. Where, educationally speaking, has the graduate come from? This is Table 6.5.
4. Where, occupationally speaking, has the graduate gone to? This is Table 6.6 and Table 6.7.

Again, while noticing the obvious risk of over-simplification, nine types of education can be distinguished and these are shown in Table 6.3. Three types of schooling are combined with three types of experience after school to produce this nine-fold classification. They ascend, in conventional British evaluations of the desirability of different educational experiences, from a non-selective schooling in an elementary, secondary modern, or comprehensive school with no education after school, to a private education in a direct grant or 'public' school followed by full-time attendance at a university. The first category accounts

Table 6.3. Types of education (each category expressed as a percentage of the whole)

School	No Further Education	Further Education	Full-time University	Total
Non-selective	25.3	41.0	0.7	67.0
Selective state	4.6	18.3	3.9	26.8
Private	0.7	3.9	1.6	6.2
				100.0

for 25.3 per cent of men in 1972, and the last for 1.6 per cent. The typical Englishman or Welshman has had a non-selective education in a state school plus some further education, usually in the form of apprenticeship or training within a firm, or part-time attendance at a technical college or night-school, or some combination of these. In the population as a whole 41 per cent are typical in this sense. The next most important group are those with some sort of selective education in a technical, central, or grammar school. The smallest groups are those who started at a non-selective school, but found their way to a university, and those who had secondary schooling in the private sector (including direct grant schools) without any education beyond school. Both of these groups constitute less than 1 per cent of the whole.

University men from all three kinds of school background amounted to 5.2 per cent of the male population in 1972. The comparable figure for those who have had a selective secondary education within the state system is 26.8 per cent and for those who went to independent schools 6.2 per cent. The numerical history of these three groups appears in the columns of Table 6.4. Of those born between 1907 and 1912, 1.5 per cent were graduates and the proportion rose steadily with a spurt (the Robbinsian expansion) for those born after 1947 to bring it up to 10.4 per cent. Private secondary schooling increased from the early years

Table 6.4. Types of education since 1907 (percentage)

Date of Birth	State Selective	Private	University
1907-12	17.2	5.2	1.5
1912-17	21.5	4.9	2.6
1917-22	26.9	5.3	2.5
1922-27	28.9	4.4	3.3
1927-32	31.4	5.9	4.3
1932-37	31.3	7.6	6.0
1937-42	28.4	7.2	7.1
1942-47	26.9	7.4	7.3
1947-52	27.8	7.1	10.4

Table 6.5. Educational origins of university men since 1907 (percentage)

Date of Birth	Type of School		
	Non-selective	Selective	Private
1907-22	30	41	29
1922-27	20	56	24
1927-32	10	55	35
1932-37	16	55	29
1937-42	13	62	25
1942-47	7	52	41
1947-52	11	62	27
All in 1972	16.5	53.1	30.4

of the century but not either fast or steadily, reaching a high point for those born just before the Second World War. Selective secondary education provided by the State followed a roughly similar course but involving proportionately four times as many people. Thus, though this is the century of educational expansion, university graduates remained in 1972 only a twentieth of the adult male population, and those with a selective education were barely a third.

How have the schools supplied the universities? (Table 6.5). Over half of the university men have come through the selective state schools that are now being reorganized as comprehensives. Rather less than a third have come from the private sector and 16.5 per cent have managed to get into the universities from a non-selective schooling.

The trends during the century have not been dramatic. Selective state schools were gradually eliminating non-selective schools as preparatory institutions for the universities, but this trend will now presumably cease. The competition, meanwhile, between the state and the private sector, has fluctuated, although indecisively.

That university graduation leads to occupational advantage is perfectly clear from column (1) of Table 6.6. Nearly nine out of every ten of the university men have found their way into the professional and managerial classes. But this is not the most interesting view of the distribution if we are looking for a meritocratic social order or some universal process of 'certification', labelling people for appropriate employment. The second column of Table 6.6 tells us more. The graduate element is still strongest at the top but nearly three-quarters of the top class are not graduates.

Table 6.6. Occupational distribution of university men

Registrar General's Class	Column (1) Percentage Distribution of University Graduates by Class	Column (2) Percentage of each class who are university graduates
I	39	27
II	48	10
III Non-manual	8	3
III Manual	3	Less than 1
IV	2	Less than 1
V	0	Less than 1
	100	

Perhaps the graduate criterion under-emphasizes the bond between education and occupation. So we return finally to the nine educational categories of Table 6.3 and show them again in Table 6.7 for the top class of professionals (the number above the diagonal in each cell) and the bottom class of unskilled workers (the number below the diagonal in each cell). The bond is clear and strong. The typical professional is a grammar-school boy with education beyond school, though not in the university. The typical unskilled worker went to an elementary or secondary modern school and no further. What presumably is happening is that the occupational hierarchy is gradually being regraded upwards in formal educational terms.

Table 6.7. Education and occupation

Registrar General's Class I (top diagonal of cells)
Registrar General's Class V (bottom diagonal of cells)
(Percentage of the occupational class with defined educational background)

School	No Further Education		Some Further Education		University	
Non-selective	1.3		18.8		3.8	
		61.0		30.4		0.0
State selective	1.2		41.5		14.6	
		5.2		2.5		0.5
Private	0.0		10.1		8.8	
		0.0		0.5		0.0

What, then, in the light of this description of the developments in education and an analysis of their relation to political aims or moral ideals, are we to make of the liberal optimisms of the twentieth century? Expansion there has been. It remains unfinished today; and along with this has been the creation of much cultural capital. But the anticipated greater equality of access to the national heritage has not materialized. Thresholds have certainly been raised and the area of free secondary education has been expanded under the auspices of the state. But the further activity of the state in expanding educational opportunity beyond the statutory leaving age has provided additional opportunities which have, at least into the 1960s, been seized disproportionately by those born into advantageous class circumstances. The overall result, on the various measures we have brought to bear, is that inequalities of class opportunity changed their form but retained their substance despite, if not indeed because of, a heavy investment by the State in enlarged educational opportunities.

In defining equality of educational opportunity however,

we have so far accepted the assumption that the characteristics of the average member of different classes were similar with respect to their claim and capacity to profit from
whatever educational opportunity society provides. We
must now question this assumption and explicitly consider
a modification of it. Merit is commonly held to constitute
a claim on social rewards and opportunities over against
the claims, for example, of citizenship or rank or market
power. Expressions of the liberal tradition in advanced industrial countries have characteristically justified the granting of opportunities to merit on grounds of efficiency in
industry, government, and administration. As governmental
bureaucracies developed in the nineteenth century, selection
of entrants on merit increasingly replaced patronage, nepo-
tism, and purchase. In Britain this movement can be traced
to colonial administration especially in India. It had a metropolitan milestone in the Northcote-Trevelyan reforms of
the Civil Service. Merit in this context was educationally
defined and the examination emerged as an instrument for
detecting potential capacity for the performance of an
expanding range of occupational positions.

   This is what is meant by the general sociological thesis
of a transition from 'ascriptive' to 'achievement' criteria in
occupational selection. The theory of meritocracy evolved
from this liberal movement and the definition attached to
it by Michael Young is summarized in the label or slogan
'IQ plus effort'. The Oxford mobility data do not yield
measures of the complex amalgam of mind and character
which would fully represent any of the possible definitions
of merit. They are confined to a definition in terms of
measured intelligence and even here the IQ distributions
between classes are estimated. Moreover, simplification
apart, the meaning of measured intelligence in the context
of explaining and justifying educational selection procedures
is highly contentious.[14] There is an unresolved debate as to
how far measured intelligence is cause and how far effect
of class membership. There is continuing disagreement as
to how far, if at all, past social selection has, in association
with assortive mating, produced *genetically* distinct classes.

The significance of class comparisons of IQ scores must accordingly be limited and tentative. Nevertheless both the method and the result of the Oxford study is of some interest. The method consists of three steps. First, the social class composition of types of school can be estimated from the 1972 survey. Second, the share of places in each type of school which would accrue to each social class if allocations were made strictly on IQ scores can also be calculated. For this second step an assumption has to be made as to the appropriate rank order of each type of school and the assumption chosen is that public schools take the highest band of IQ. Then third, the actual shares are compared with the hypothetical IQ or 'meritocratic' shares obtained by each class in each type of school. The result turns out to be that the real world and the hypothetical meritocratic world are pretty similar. Moreover, this closeness of fit has been characteristic of secondary schooling for the past half century.

However, a crucially different result emerges when the same kind of analysis is applied to education beyond the statutory school-leaving age. Here the queue is reconstituted to give the universities the first slice of measured intelligence, the colleges of education the second, and part-time further education the third. When the quota which would have been allocated to each class in each birth cohort on IQ measurement is set alongside the actual allocation, it emerges that there was class equality of opportunity on meritocratic assumptions for some form of post-secondary education. But in the case of the most sought-after form of education beyond school—the university—there was still class inequality between the middle class and the other two classes. Privileged, that is non-meritocratic, access to the universities rose to its highest point among those born between 1933 and 1942, and then fell back, but not quite to the point recorded for the first cohort of those born between 1913 and 1922. Lower middle-class boys born after the Second World War were relatively disadvantaged compared with their predecessors after the First World War, while working-class boys stayed at much the same level of relative disadvantage in the 1960s as they had been after the First World War, and with even more disadvantage in the years between. Thus, paradoxically, if the university is regarded as the crowning edifice of the State's policy of educational expansion, it is ironic to notice that this is the development which accords least with the meritocratic principle.

Though the study on which I have relied cannot tell us what effect, if any, has ensued from the further development of comprehensive secondary schooling and polytechnics since 1972, I see no reason to suppose that any marked change in the social distribution of educational *achievement* has been taking place over the most recent five years. It is true, of course, that comprehensive reorganization and abolition of the direct grant schools brought the vast majority of secondary as well as primary schoolchildren under one educational roof, leaving a minority of 5 per cent of children, mostly from rich families, in an increasingly isolated private sector with privileges which are difficult to defend. But the geographical distribution of the social classes and the subtleties of the interaction between school and family, which result in a continuing association of class origin with education destination, still defy the declared intent of governments to secure what a Conservative Minister of Education, Sir Edward (later Lord) Boyle, described as 'the essential point . . . that all children should have an equal opportunity of acquiring intelligence, and of developing their talents and abilities to the full.'[15] Serious intent along these lines would require policies and resources of positive discrimination which no British government has so far contemplated.

The long words of politics—capitalism, socialism, communism, and democracy—have many and ambiguous meanings. So too, has the educational system appropriate to a modern society. Education prepares children for society, transforming biological organisms into social personalities. Its capacity is essentially not to create but to recreate society, not to form structures of social life but to maintain the people and the skills that inform these structures. Education as a means of social change is secondary. It is not impotent because, *pace* Marx/Engels, man's social consciousness to some degree determines his social existence. Yet that social existence must be the starting point for reforming educational policies of the past which come out of a class society, evolving perhaps towards one of classless inequality, complicated by the peculiar British history of political independence, of cultural homogeneity, and of primacy in the development of an urban-industrial civilization.

Ideologically, the national histories of education seem also to have echoed the themes with which we are concerned in this book—liberty, equality, and fraternity—against the constraining forces of structure and culture in each country. In Britain, the constraints have been those of a class society which gave rise, in the nineteenth century, to a mass system of elementary education imposed from above. Liberty gave ideological justification to the privileges of the minority in the public schools and the Oxford colleges, and later to an enlarged minority through selective secondary schools and universities. For the mass it was essentially freedom for a selected few to escape—a policy of selective educational embourgeoisment. This, at the same time, was the liberal approach to equality, taking the form of policies of equality of opportunity. Liberty also increasingly penetrated the infant school in that brief period in the life of a child in which there is some protection from the exigencies of educational selection. Thus, the twentieth century debate in education has been dominated by a liberal solution which links equality to liberty but, with the exception of the comprehensive school movement, neglects the link to fraternity.

Let me, to conclude this chapter and to adumbrate the general directions for which I shall plead in the final chapter, consider what kind of educational policy would put fraternity into more even balance with liberty and equality. The liberal approach through slow and limited expansion would not be enough. The equality of plenitude is probably an unattainable dream. We are unlikely to see the Utopia, which William Morris envisaged in *News from*

Nowhere,[16] of a consensual restriction of consumer demands together with happy coincidences between demand and voluntary supply of services. Nor can there be firm reliance on the American hope for unrestricted supply through technological advance leading to rates of economic growth which out-distance consumer expectations. In reality, a balanced educational policy would have to deal with the equality of scarcity—which means educationally the problems of transformation from élite to mass, rather than mass to universal higher education. Such a policy is therefore bound to hurt the established vested interests of privileged minorities. Moreover, to reassert an unpalatable truth, equality can never be attained through educational policies alone.

But making the large assumption that a society which wanted equality would put through the necessary fundamental reforms for the equalization of participation in the work place and the community, the structure of schooling would be that of recurrent education, and rights of participation in it would be those of citizenship rather than those of the market-place. The selective function of education for a hierarchy of occupational positions would be transformed into one of differentiation for a complex and fluid array of jobs having roughly equal material rewards. Selection would thereby become strictly educational.

The allocation of resources to education in such a system would not substitute flat equality for the present unequal reinforcement of advantages already distributed to families in a hierarchy of class and status. It would follow the principle of positive discrimination directed against all arbitrary or accidental, and therefore unfair, disadvantages. This would mean less for the universities and more for the nurseries, less for Solihull and more for Newham, less for the eighteen to twenty-one year-olds and more for the over sixty-fives. The basic citizenship right to a given amount of time free from work would be universal, and its increments would accrue to everyone and not simply to those in the rising generation. This basic citizenship principle would then be linked to, and modified by, that of positive discrimination through carefully worked out and constantly revised formulas for translating measures of disadvantage into extra eduational benefits in so far as these were not more appropriately dealt with through income, employment, and housing policies.

In the interests of fraternity both the organization and content of education would be centred on the idea of community schools. At all levels education would be locally governed within the national framework of citizenship right and positive discrimination. The form of educational government would be participatory democracy, within which the role of the professional teacher would be that of community servant with all this implies for teacher training, the practice of educational administration, and the claims of teachers' unions. 'Free schools' would find their place in such a community organization, and might, incidentally, offer a more effective service of experiment and innovation than was ever given by the 'public schools'.

The idea of the community school has to be given a geographical meaning, especially for the under-fives, parents, and over sixty-fives. In part, this would be to recognize the hidden costs of alienation, anomie, rootlessness, and isolation which are exchanged for the benefits of physical mobility. In part, it would be to recognize the costs in inhumanity of grandiose economic and political structures. In part, it would be to assert that in so far as there is a 'logic of industrialism', it does not necessarily involve the rates of migration which are presently experienced, and far less the destruction of local social networks by mindless urban planning. Educationally, it would be to assert the learning potential of all social relations and to deny the arbitrary attribution of monopoly to the formal teacher in the classroom. Culturally, it would be to assert the worth of local life, its distinctiveness, and its commonalities with other places and other times, and to deny that local experience only fosters parochialism and excludes universalism.

Higher education would become adult education, and in that sense immediately be made universal. Its organization would also be dominated by the idea of the community school, and its development would realize the principles of recurrent education. There would thus be a greater variety and flexibility of provision in community colleges and local institutions, as well as through the mass media and the Open University. Access and student finance would be provided through sabbaticals and arrangements for retirement.

What, it may be asked, would then become of the privileges enjoyed by a Fellow of Nuffield College? An answer is given by a fable concerning an alternative history for Oxford. An aristocrat and a Franciscan, travelling together in search of education, came to the banks of the Cherwell. 'Have you', said the aristocrat, 'any coinage about you?' The monk searched the folds of his habit and produced a florin which the aristocrat flipped nonchalantly into the river. 'Come now', he said 'let us enter this town like gentlemen.' The population of that town was never large, and its style of life was ascetic: but its science, scholarship, and social criticism was known, influential, and respected throughout the land.

7   The basis of social order

It is perfectly possible that the United Kingdom of England, Scotland, Wales, and Northern Ireland will shortly disintegrate. Even to say this in 1978 may be thought sacrilegious: and to have said it ten years ago would have been to be dismissed as absurd. But if for a moment we look beyond native British pieties and take instead the wider perspective of contemporary world history, the prospect of an approaching insular disestablishment becomes rather commonplace. Integration between nations and ethnic disintegration within them is the common pattern of current economic and political development all over the world. The British find themselves drawn simultaneously into the European Economic Community and into Scottish and Welsh separatism. The very different political and economic circumstances of the Russian Empire, of China, and of Africa reveal on a larger scale in each case the same story. Enlarging economic organization, with modernity as its aim, combines with sharp internal conflicts between Russian and non-Russian within the U.S.S.R., Han and non-Han minorities in China, and tribal groups in Africa.[1] The British experience is not unique. Nor is conflict, despite a cultural bias against recognizing it, in any way odd. As I pointed out in Chapter 1, the coexistence of interests and scarcity make it more difficult to explain why societies hang together, rather than why they break up.

All the more, then, is it a puzzle that, at least since Culloden in 1746, despite the alarm and dramas of the revolutionary years of 1688 and 1848, and the General strike of 1926, and notwithstanding the Southern Irish breakaway in 1922, and the current so-called troubles which we hesitate to name as civil war, British history and the British State have been quite outstandingly tranquil. Ever since the battle between the Parliamentary armies and the forces of the Crown, more than three hundred years ago, the outstanding fact about Britain is domestic peace. Apologists throughout the modern age and down to our own day have never tired of words like 'decency', 'tolerance', and 'restraint', and phrases like 'respect for tradition', 'innate conservatism', 'the law and the constitution', and so on through a political and social lexicon of approval for consensus and condemnation of 'extremism'. However, unlike those of consensus, the ugly words of political conflict never rid themselves of their inverted commas. 'Capitalism' and 'communism', 'bourgeoisie' and 'bureaucrat', 'dialectic' and 'demarche', 'liberation' and 'liquidation': these remain alien visitors to an unfanatical tradition of political discourse. Not only in tourist brochures is the essential England still depicted as curling wood-smoke from a Cotswold cottage against an autumn sky.

Why? How did the nation that led the industrial revolution somehow contrive this changelessness? How did it retain monarchic and medieval symbols of unity, absorb first a bourgeoisie and second a proletariat, turn Hadrian's Wall and the Edwardian castles into tourist attractions, and contain the Eisteddfod (which, I am told, is a medieval invention of the nineteenth century) and the kilt as quaint atavistic regional colourfulness, signifying politically nothing? And why, if it is so, are these ancient manifestations of war, bloodshed, force and oppression, so long turned into harmless symbols of pacification and gentleness, now re-emerging as signals of separatism and hostility? These are the final questions for this book: the problem of fraternity which has been latent in my discussion of liberty and equality, the problem of social order which has underlain my chronicle of class, status, and party.

One thing is obvious. Neither Marxism nor liberalism by itself can solve the central problem—the problem of order or, as I have put it, fraternity. Neither tradition ever developed a serious theory of nationalism. For the Marxist nationalism is a secondary force, more or less useful in the march of history towards world revolution, given greater or lesser emphasis according to whether the theorist prefers Lenin or Rosa Luxemburg.[2] Liberal theory, too, has a central concept of one world, evolving as rationality displaces mercantilism and other superstitions towards free trade, patterned by comparative cost advantages. Both theories come out of the early development of capitalism, both vastly over-estimate the possibility of economic solutions—the Marxists by assuming that the economic power of the capitalist class is all that stands in the way of a harmonious society of free and equal men, needing no political state to organize their brotherhood; the liberals, by assuming that the free market generates just distribution, needing only minimal government to guard its contractual perfection.

I want to argue that there are native traditions of social and political theory, which can be of more use to those who search for a solution. If the first enemy of social peace in Britain is the persistence of inequality, then we can look to such writers as T. H. Marshall who, as I suggested in the third chapter, avoids both the Marxist and the liberal error. He stands in a tradition much influenced by Durkheim and Weber. He brings us back to politics as the arena in which the conflicting claims of class and status are fought out. As David Lockwood has pointed out,[3] his theory of citizenship offers the most cogent answer to the problem, originally posed by Durkheim, of the basis of solidarity in modern societies.

Social Integration in Modern Society

Writing in 1893,[4] Durkheim distinguished two forms of solidarity. The first type he called 'segmental', and the second 'organic'. In pre-literate societies, solidarity is mechanical, based on substitutability and resemblance. Individuals have experience and feelings common to all. The social units of society are also similar in form and function, each family being much like any other family in the society, and each community like every other community. As society advances, it comes to depend increasingly on the division of labour. Individuals are differentiated in their feelings. They are bound together now, not by consciousness of kind, but by their interdependence, their complementarity. The question then becomes: what is the social base for organic solidarity in modern societies. Durkheim's general answer need not detain us. But before we leave him, we can note that he made an acute observation concerning late nineteenth century Britain.

It may very well happen, that in a particular society a certain division of labour—and especially economic division of labour—may be highly developed, while the segmental type may still be rather pronounced. This certainly seems to be the case in England: major industry, big business, appears to be as highly developed there as on the continent, while the segmental system is still very much in evidence, as witness both the autonomy of local life, and the authority retained by tradition.

Local autonomy and the strength of tradition are two clues to the maintainance of social integration in Britain, despite marked inequalities of class and status. And we can add the further Durkheimian point (though one he did not specifically apply to England) that 'all external inequality compromises organic solidarity'.[5] Writers like Barbara Wootton, Ralph Dahrendorf, John Goldthorpe, R. H. Titmuss, and Alan Fox have carried further T. H. Marshall's approach to a direct analysis of the relation between inequality and social integration, and I shall return to them.[6]

Societies in general are made and broken by like interests leading to cohesion or competition, and by unlike interests which bind men together or bring them into conflict. But there is another principle of social organization—domination—which has become increasingly important in modern societies in the form of the authority of rationally created rules. Authority always has two sides, force and faith: the faith of the ruled that the rulers have the right to make rules by which people must live (for example, that they must pay such-and-such amounts in taxes), and the force that the rulers have at their disposal to compel compliance with the rules. In modern societies, by far the most important source of authoritative rules is the State, and the definition of the State, at once most simple and most useful, is that it has a monopoly of ultimate force in the territory it claims. But societies are not identical with States, as the example of Scotland clearly shows. The integration of a society is based less on force and more on faith—that is, on cultural affinities of language, custom, belief, and history, which give the members a consciousness of kind and kin with each other, and a sense of cultural boundary from other peoples. These bonds are more enduring so that states and empires have risen and fallen more rapidly than have societies: a nation and people can live, politically or militarily speaking, underground through many generations of foreign rule. Faith converts force into authority and consent.

But faith may vary in its social bases. It may be engendered or maintained by the power of classes, status groups, or parties to influence the consciousness of those they dominate. Consequently, some may wish to distinguish a third force, and to label it 'fraud'. Fraud typically resides in the power of ruling groups to exercise calculated control over communication, and thus to impose ideas and beliefs on the majority in the interests of the minority. In this way, organized religion, schooling, and the mass media may serve to hold a society together, continually reinforcing and disseminating its established ideologies. In practice, integration by fraud is intrinsically fragile. False faith is more characteristically an unintended consequence of unequally shared power. Conspiracy theories of society cannot be convincingly applied to Britain, and those writers like Dr. Parkin who interpret the problem of social order as essentially that of legitimating the control of a dominant class, nonetheless recognize a variety of social mechanisms, such as religious ritual, the teaching of school history, or opportunities for social mobility, as *not* deliberate creations of that dominant class.[7]

Yet, given force, faith, or fraud, the frailty of authority

remains a central problem of large and complex modern societies. Three types of authority were distinguished in Chapter 4. One of these, the rational-legal in Max Weber's inelegant phrase, bids to dominate the modern world in the form of *bureaucracy*. What is rational and legal about this type of authority is that it claims to apply to particular cases. Its deeper justification comes, at least in Britain, from the fact (or at least the theory) that the general rules are arrived at by democratic legislation. It rests ultimately on the preferences of the majority. The danger is that bureaucrats all too easily and frequently break the chain from popular will to executive decision.

There is a second type of authority—*charisma*—the personal authority of the inspired leader who is trusted by his followers. His word is the criterion of truth and worth. This type of authority also has its frailties. Those who have it, like Mao Tse Tung, must one day die. Those who aspire to it, like James Callaghan or David Steel, must face the ordeal of their Annual Party conferences. And there is a third type—tradition. Today's orders are justified on the grounds that we have always done it that way. It is ancestral wisdom. But I hardly need to explain the frailty of traditional authority in our world of rapid social change. In the village where I grew up, custom decreed that all adults, within limits well understood, could and should act *in loco parentis*. There was a inter-generational authority. But in the shifting populations of large cities, young people are less ready to accord respect to their elders. 'Grandad' becomes a term of contempt. This is the absence of inter-generational authority.

It seems almost, once one's thoughts begin to run on these lines, that the newspapers, the radio, and the television are concerned with nothing else than authority, the conditions for its exercise, and the causes of its rupture. Car workers rampage through the management canteen at the Ford plant, young men assault old women in the street, prisoners rebel against warders in the gaols, condemned members of the Irish Republican Army refuse to recognize an Irish court.

By way of contrast, I recently saw a copy of a passport signed by Lord Palmerston in 1851.[8]

We, Henry John Viscount Palmerston, Baron Temple, a Peer of Ireland, a Member of Her Britannic Majesty's Most Honourable Privy Council, a Member of Parliament, Knight Grand Cross of the most Honorable Order of the Bath, Her Majesty's Principal Secretary of State for Foreign Affairs, request and require in the Name of Her Majesty all those whom it may concern to allow Mr. Edward Holyroyd, his wife, Mrs. Holyroyd, two daughters and three sons, travelling on the Continent, with a man and a maid servant, to pass freely without let or hindrance, and to afford them every assistance and protection of which they may stand in need. Given at the Foreign Office, London, the 10th day of July 1851.

Notice the symbols of authority here. And, perhaps even more telling, the confident description of social hierarchy from Her Majesty down through the Viscount to Mr. Holyroyd and thence to sons and daughters, and finally a man and a maid servant.

Honi soit qui mal y pense, says the heraldry. No matter that, three years before, Marx and Engels in the Communist Manifesto of 1848 had, with no less confidence, announced the impending fall of the capitalist state, the overthrow of imperial authority by the rising revolutionary proletariat.

In 1976 I read, in the *Daily Mirror,* Geoffrey Goodman's brilliant tabloid history of the twentieth-century rise of *new* authorities—the TUC, and the Parliamentary Labour Party—from Downing Street, Manchester, to Downing Street, London, to become what journalists now describe as the natural government of the country. But Goodman ended his account with a remark about the Annual Conferences, that they were a much-cherished opportunity for the rank and file to belabour their masters on the platform, rather as we know many primitive tribes have annual rituals in which the chief is ceremoniously reviled and insulted by licensed warriors before the assembled people.

On the next day we learned that Mr. Callaghan had disciplined one of his Cabinet colleagues, Reg Prentice (who has since joined the Conservative Party) for 'rocking the boat' with a speech hostile to the proposed Labour policy programme. Meanwhile, news continued to come in from China about bitter struggles for succession to the places emptied by death among the founding gerontocracy of that regime.

I choose these diverse examples partly to emphasize that the problem of authority is ubiquitous in human relationships, extending from the encounter in the street through those small human groups which are sufficiently bound by rules for us to call them institutions, like the family, or the youth club, or the office, and on up to the great political organizations of party and parliament.

From all these instances, we can discern the three basic forms of authority—rational-legal, charismatic, and traditional—combining and contending with one another. And we can further see that social change makes each of them uncertain as sources for stable and peaceable relations between people. The examples emphasize that authority is not a synonym for law. The adults in my village had no legal authority over children: but they had the authority of long-established tradition. Callaghan had no legal control over Prentice's expression of opinion, but he too had the sanction of tradition—the fraternal solidarity of the platform—plus, and perhaps more effective, the power of a prime minister to exclude people from his cabinet. Neither law nor traditional authority is absolute. The young 'mugger' flouts the law and prime minsterial power could not silence Prentice. Perhaps Callaghan could have dominated his wayward colleague by sheer force of the other type of authority—charisma. Certainly Mao exercised enormous charisma in his progress from young revolutionary in Yenan Province to the chairmanship in Peking. But charisma too has no universal writ. It may be routinized, as with Christ's authority in the institution of the papal succession. But Mao's charisma, if it did not die with him, at least could not prevent a power struggle among the survivors.

Charisma is historically like the wind which bloweth where it listeth. Churchill is thought of in Britain as having had this type of authority. He gained it at a moment of desperate external threat to a country at war. External threat does, in fact, accelerate the process whereby many are called and few are chosen. Present conditions seem to approach a somewhat similar intensity of threatened collapse. But let us be clear that the possibility of new and dramatic leadership, which infirmity invites, is highly dangerous. Charisma is no necessary friend of democracy— *explicitly* not if it comes from the political extreme Right, and *actually* not if it comes from the extreme Left, for all its ideological clothing in rhetoric proclaiming the will of the people.

If neither charisma nor rational legality are adequate bases for a viable authority, the only other recourse is to tradition: and the central political tradition in Britain is democracy. Democracy is the consensus of free men, free to assemble, to express opinion, to persuade, and to elect, but, having done so, willing to accept the will of the majority whose rule will be tempered by consideration for the minority among whom they may at any time find themselves. Democracy is not a long tradition. It was a usurper at the end of the eighteenth century, fighting a previous tradition of feudal custom. As I pointed out in Chapter 4, it was slow in coming. It has yet to be fully realized beyond the formalities of the polling booth in those spheres of life, particularly the work place, where it lays claim to be applied.

I am not, of course, suggesting that democracy can be applied mechanically to all forms of human association. What I am suggesting is that it can be the ultimate court of appeal for our secular lives. Families cannot be full democracies: they are not bands of brothers, and the lesser responsibility of childhood is an inescapable fact: but they can be, and can be judged as, nurseries of responsible citizenship. Schools and universities cannot be democracies, whatever is said by the National Union of Students. If you are a teacher and I come to learn, then your knowledge must have authority over my ignorance: but again, the school you run is successful precisely in so far as it brings me to competent citizenship in the trade, profession, or subject you teach me; and from that moment I can claim the right to democratic relations with you.

That is all obvious enough. But Britain is far from laying

the democratic foundation for traditional authority in all the spheres to which its modern evolution points. There are two spheres of life where this is conspicuously so—the nation state and industrial organization—two areas in which the democratic principle could be more firmly applied.

The starting point in both spheres is that a modern society organizes itself by extremely specialized division of labour. But in national affairs Britain has overreached itself. It is tied into a huge apparatus of international markets. It has given over a great deal of its effective authority to international agencies through membership of the E.E.C., the development of multi-national companies, and its trading relations all over the world. And the island occupies a specialist position within this complex through the London money market which we call the City. Britain is very far from being an autonomous economy and, quite apart from internal dissension, the extent to which its government can control inflation, price levels, and standards of life is feeble. To domesticate authority within its shores—and so to give its people a chance to run an effective democracy—would probably entail some cost to their general standard of living.

Some would prefer to pay that material price, assuming democratic justice in the distribution of the burden: and it must be pointed out in defence of this 'little Englandism' that no economist or politician in the current debate who seeks solutions within the international framework holds out any immediate prospect of relieving the misery of a million-and-a-half unemployed. That is one painful and inequitably distributed cost of persistence with the large and therefore effectively undemocratic system under which Britons live.

I said, 'quite apart from internal dissension'. That brings me to the other sphere in which greater democratization is possible, and here I would point to the analyses offered by Alan Fox. Fox's main attention in *Beyond Contract*[9] is focused on the experience of work in the office, the factory, and the workshop. Work relations in the past have given low discretion and low trust to subordinates *vis-à-vis* their superiors. This was the triumph of the so-called scientific management which reached its most extreme form in the modern factory assembly line. The low-discretion syndrome, as Fox describes it, contrasts the rank and file production worker with the professional. The worker on the shop floor has little sense of being an expert; of commitment to a calling; of autonomy on the job; of obligation to produce high-quality work, and he has little or no sense of identification with the organization in which he works.

Fox has also analysed the low levels of trust which lie behind the struggles between different groups of organized workers. Obviously a more democratically integrated society would organize its work by the opposite principles of high-trust relations, both vertically and horizontally. Professional work at its best requires and involves a high level of trust between people. Rigidly hierarchical forms of industrial authority produce at best the solidarity of the resentful.

Industrial democracy is a vital element in the unfinished British programme of creating a society which commands willing and widespread allegiance. Like Fox, I do not go far with those who announce the arrival of the corporate society as the new Leviathan. British evolution has strong roots in liberal individualism, and little or nothing in those Hegelian or organic conceptions of society which see the individual and his purposes as having meaning only in terms of corporate membership. Indeed, Britain has the strongest shop-steward organization in the world. Its indiscipline against corporatism is far more impressive than the corporative hierarchy of the Trades Union Council, which the mass media are quick to portray as the modern demon. What is more important than shop-steward radicalism is that this shop-floor organization is the most conspicuous form of democracy in contemporary Britain. Nevertheless, the low discretion, low trust principle still dominates work organization.

These tendencies could, however, be reversed. Reversal, of course, might carry its considerable price—and not only in terms of cars and television sets (at least in a transitional period). But estimates of that price must be examined with scepticism when they come from those with a private interest in maintaining the *status quo*. 'Scientific management' methods are not invariably the most efficient. Doubts as to whether 'bigness is best' are to be found among hard-headed industrialists, as well as among idealist proponents of the view that 'small is beautiful'. Earlier in the century Sidney and Beatrice Webb were more powerful advocates of the idea of consumer co-operatives than was G. D. H. Cole as the champion of producer co-operatives. But producer co-operatives are now attracting serious attention from those, of diverse political persuasions, who find planning and control by centralized bureaucracies unpromising for fraternity. Evidence from the thriving Mandragone producer co-operatives in the Basque provinces of Spain suggests strongly that this form of management makes for more rather than less efficiency. Any argument that extension of high-trust relations must be at the expense of the expectation of affluence needs to be qualified by realistic appraisal of a country's particular conditions. However, there seems little doubt that some price would have to be paid. Moreover, there is little prospect of the bargain being eagerly sought either by those presently in authority (who have vested interests in their present power), or the workers, patients, consumers, and citizens (who are conditioned to prefer a bit more of what material benefits they already have). Only those who experience autonomy and relations of trust can fully appreciate their satisfactions.

The Forces of Fusion and Fission

Yet despite the frailty of authority and the insecurity of consensus which these examples illustrate, no Hobbesian collapse of civil society has so far marred modern British history. On the contrary, force and faith in their varied manifestations, have played their part in what has been, historically, a remarkably United Kingdom. The twentieth-century inheritance was, on balance, heavily weighted towards fusion rather than fission. Some of the unifying influences are easy enough to discern. The British State, centred on the Crown in Parliament, held undisputed sway over England, Scotland, and Wales for two centuries and, more important, naval power controlled an Empire eventually covering one-quarter of the land surface of the whole earth. Britain in 1900 was still the greatest of imperial nations, a major workshop of the world, and miraculously secured at the same time by a still impregnable insularity. British society was itself the apex of a world-wide imperial dominion, and London the financial centre of world trade.

This powerful combination of industry and empire obviously afforded huge wealth and wide opportunity to its controllers. Wealth and opportunity were most unequally shared within the society, between classes, sexes, and regions. But continuing, if decelerating and unsteady expansion, itself a supplement to integration, was further and massively reinforced by the custom and culture of a most peculiar island. It was a culture of patrician liberalism. The aristocracy and the gentry maintained a dominance over both society and State from the overthrow of absolutist monarchy in the seventeenth century, and right through the imperial and industrial developments of the next two hundred years. The continuity of cultural symbols—a constitutional monarch, a tame but titled Second Chamber, a democratized but dignified Oxford and Cambridge—was made possible by these economic and military forces and, in turn, gave venerated changelessness to the continuous adaptiveness of a dominant class.

So, as Tom Nairn has put it, and is, in effect, saying what Durkheim said:

the pioneer modern liberal-constitutional state never itself became modern: it retained the archaic stamp of its priority. Later the industrialization which it produced, equally pioneering and equally world-wide in impact, never made England into a genuinely industrialized society . . . And therefore no recovery from industrial 'backwardness' has been possible, precisely because no second revolution of the state has taken place in England: only the state could have engendered such a recovery, by revolution from above—but the old patrician structure of England's political system, incapable of such radical action, has also resisted every effort at serious reform up to the present day.[10]

But, I would add, if economically weak, it was made socially strong by the culture of the gentleman.

Nairn's historical analysis has to be taken seriously. Liberalism as a theory of free markets in the service of economic growth is older in England than the bourgeois industrialist manufacturer. The English land-owning classes had developed it long before the industrial revolution.[11] The aristocracy and the gentry absorbed the bourgeoisie in the nineteenth century. This gave to the twentieth century a stratified society which, though strongly resembling the Marxist description of polarized class society if one looked at the northern industrial towns, was also a status hierarchy of apparent agelessness. It was rooted in a medieval agrarian past. It provided a governing class descended from pre-industrial times to which was added, especially in the southern counties, those whose wealth and status derived from the Empire, and from the finance capitalism of the City of London.

In short, Edwardian Britain was a country of inequality, but a strongly knit nation. A legacy of feudal aristocracy had, in the course of overseas imperialism and domestic industrialization, been accepted by both bourgeoisie and proletariat. No wonder, then, that Lord David Cecil saw the sunset over his grandfather's deathbed as also the twilight of British greatness. For the fusion I have briefly sketched was gradually to be dissolved by corrosion at home and abroad. The industrial competitors abroad—American and Germany—had already ended Britain's pre-eminence. In a century of relative, though not absolute, decline there was a period of prosperity in the 1950s and '60s. When that interlude ended, domestic discontents fanned by economic stagnation, class and status inequalities, and more recently the recrudescence of older nationalisms, were less and less easily contained by the traditional remedies of political liberalism, gentlemanly culture, and civic incorporation. A formidable toll of human energy and resource now has to be mobilized in order to control a country hitherto frequently held up as an examplar of urbane peace. On a Saturday in February 1978, five thousand

policemen were drafted into the East London constituency
of Ilford to prevent clashes between the National Front and
its opponents. In Northern Ireland at the same time there
were thirty-one thousand British soldiers, making a ratio of
one to every forty-five of the population. This is a ratio
not very different to that of teachers to schoolchildren
before the Second World War.

Nevertheless, there have been strong forces making for
integration. If only because we are so accustomed now to
gloomy discussion of Britain's economic decline, we should
remind ourselves that it is a country for which this century
has been one of economic growth. True, no enormous reliance can be placed on the national book-keeping of economists which suggests a tripling of real income per head since
1900. There is what I have called 'the other economy'
which runs from intra-familial services to the cash payments
without receipts of the moonlighter. But growth there has
most certainly been, and the average person is unquestionably better fed, better clothed, better housed, and enjoys
a longer, healthier, and more leisured life than his Edwardian predecessor. Clearly allegiance to a society is more
secure when these ameliorations are in train, that is, when
the generations see a darker past and a brighter future.

We also do well to remind ourselves of the integrating
aspects of war. It is a paradox of external conflict that it
promotes equality and fraternity within the nation. This
is true especially of modern 'total' war. If all must be called
upon to fight for their country, all must be brought to
believe that they have a stake in it. Both World Wars brought
renewed promise for the future. They reinforced patriotic
sentiment.

> But ever 'twixt the book and his bright eyes
> The gleaming eagles of the legions came.[12]

This was possible reverie for a young clerk in England in
the First World War and even the Second, before the bomb
dropped on Hiroshima. The two Wars also softened class
divisions and reduced inequality. In 1945, much more
than in 1919, there was intense feeling among working

men and women that the promises of English culture were about to be redeemed in their own lives. As they had sung in the shadows, so now they sang Edward Carpenter's secular hymn in the light: England is risen and day is here.

Yet, although war and prosperity may tend to integrate, other twentieth-century experiences have had an opposite effect. For one thing, economic growth has had a cyclical character. Earlier slumps were increasingly forgotten in the full employment decades of the 1950s and '60s. But their failure seriously to disturb the social and political order in the 1930s is testimony only to the power of cultural integration. As we have seen, when he came to Jarrow in 1933, J. B. Priestley marvelled that men in such economic conditions, not under the constraint of military force, but on the contrary politically enfranchized, should nevertheless have accepted their lot.[13] That they did has to be explained largely by the strength of a consensual political culture. It inculcated belief in progress towards a more civilized society and nourished the faith that as their cause was just, so their victory was certain.

Again, industrial productivity in the twentieth century has been accompanied by growing alienation of labour. On his inter-war journey, Priestley reports the opinion of a craftsman that 'all our labour troubles did not come from a quarrel about distribution of the profits, but from a deeper cause, the crushing of the workman's self respect by mechanical labour in which he could not find himself'.[14] And the author returns to the theme in reflecting on a Leicester sock-making factory. He remarks the 'great distinction between the fortunate few who are outside the machine and are capable of making changes in it and the great mass of ordinary work people, mostly women, who are inside the machine, simply part of it. This distinction is so great that you feel that the two sets of people ought to belong to two different races.[15] Of those 'inside the machine' he observes 'they are not bullied or even nagged at; their very weaknesses are elaborately taken into account; their comfort is considered, but between the time when they 'clock in' and 'clock out' their central human dignity which entitles them under our democratic system to a vote as good as anybody else's, has no real existence, except in that dream of life which occupies their minds as their fingers fly to do their own mysterious little task.'[16]

But above all—the factor of paramount importance—has been the essentially unprincipled inequality of distribution of wealth and income. The stubborn persistence of distributional inequality of wealth and income up to 1970 needs no further documentation. And it is true that, at least until recently, the implications of inequality have manifested themselves in the economic rather than the political sphere. Within the economic sphere, however—in industrial relations and the management of incomes policy—inequality has been corrosive. The manifestations have not been those of class warfare but rather, as John Goldthorpe has argued, 'in a situation of anomie; that is . . . a lack of moral regulation over the wants and goals that individuals hold'.[17] Consensual politics have been maintained partly by the remarkably restricted comparisons within and between classes which Runciman has analysed,[18] and partly by the political culture of democracy which I reviewed in Chapter 4.

However, the development of the social rights of citizenship generates conflict as well as consensus in such a way as to *exacerbate* anomic conditions. This unintended by-product of an otherwise integrative force takes at least three forms. First the egalitarian principle intrinsic to citizenship challenges normative approval of market inequalities. Class and citizenship are at war in the twentieth century. Second, citizenship also undermines traditional status hierarchies which, though strongly rooted in British culture, are conventionally, not legally, based. Citizenship is therefore a basis for dissent from the established social order. And third, the extension of citizenship rights into the industrial sphere—a movement towards various forms of industrial democracy—gives unions, and especially local groups of workers and their shop stewards, increased protection and power to pursue their market and work interests relatively undisciplined by traditional constraints.

So, the partial development of the principle of citizenship, under circumstances where competing distributional principles deriving from class, status, and citizenship still contend for pre-eminence, may reduce rather than increase organic solidarity. The consequences have been increasingly evident in the recent history of industrial relations. They are most dramatically illustrated in the growing bitterness of race relations in the major English cities.

It is always an open question, of course, how far economic inequality, alienation, and anomie take on political forms of expression. They may be individualized or localized. Rising rates of crime, vandalism, and hooliganism are possible outcomes: and these have risen markedly in recent decades. The connections, I must emphasize, are not proven. Nonetheless, whatever the reason for the escalation of antisocial activity, there can be no doubt that they in turn reduce confidence in the political and social order. The legitimacy of government and administration is thereby threatened. The apparently increasing frequency of corruption in government and administration—or perhaps simply the wider publicity it receives from investigative journalism—further diminishes civic trust. We cannot measure exactly the strength of these forces, and I fully appreciate that political corruption is normal rather than abnormal in the history of states. Nevertheless, solidarity in Britain in the nineteenth and early twentieth centuries has depended heavily on political trust to counterbalance resentments naturally born of inequality.

The Shifting Balance of Cohesion and Conflict

Twentieth-century experience, then, has been mixed. Before the First World War, discontents springing from class divisions and stultifying industrial labour were checked by limited working-class expectations and the strong alliance of aristocrat and bourgeois. Meanwhile, the old traditions of civil liberty in which modern citizenship is rooted, though providing the legal basis for the development of class inequalities, had also begun to extend into political enfranchisement and into a set of social rights which later came to be called the Welfare State. The organization of the working class was also built on the same foundations of citizenship. These integrative forces were, however, only weakly struggling into existence, and they carried their own threats to the established order. There was also, especially on Clydeside, a serious syndicalist current flowing away from the more moderate mainstream of the Trade Unions, the Co-operative Societies, and the infant Labour Party. The war itself suspended opposition and brought a primitive form of war socialism, some reduction of wage differentials, and steps towards the emancipation of women.

Return to 'normalcy', as it was then termed, shifted the balance again towards, but not quite back to, the pre-war situation. Religion had lost some of its restraining power. The expected boundaries of self-fulfilment were pushed back, educational horizons began to widen, and many intellectuals were vehemently critical of bourgeois life and values. This was the period of fellow travelling (see p.98). Nevertheless, this weakening of cultural control never showed sings of being turned into a threatening political movement. British radical politics centred on the Labour Party. Bitter industrial struggles scarred the 1920s, but the rise of the Labour Party after the First World War to replace the Liberal Party was its incorporation into the politics of consensus, not very different from that described in the nineteenth century by Walter Bagehot. Then the slump years of the early 1930s temporarily overlaid the basic politics of belief in progress with hopelessness, fatalism, and fragmentation—a deadening and defeatist interpretation of events was universally shared: economic depression was seen as externally imposed rather than politically soluble.

Then again, partial recovery and the Second World War eased the tensions and renewed the national promise. Liberty, equality, and fraternity all made progress during the war and post-war years. Labour Party philosophy dominated politics and there were even five early post-war years of a Labour Government in clear majority—winning the solid allegiance of most of those who came of political age in the 1930s and 1940s. The Labour victory was never, the British reputation for incorruptible government. The industrial working class. But, in any case, the following thirteen years of Conservative government were years of full employment, and of educational and occupational opportunity for a significant minority of the new generation of the working class. Belief in an emergent meritocracy was developing in this period, despite the evidence of continuing class inequality of conditions for fair competition, which are necessary for meritocratic principles to replace hereditary or ascriptive ones as the normative basis for an unequal society. It was a time of high net upward mobility and of slowly burgeoning mass affluence. The tide of political consensus flowed strongly for twenty years or more.

The tide turned yet again in the 1960s. By this time the Empire was gone. Ideologically, all that was left was Powellite English nationalism. Economically, what remained was the overseas-oriented financial capitalism of the City, which drained talent and attention away from the needs of an ageing and sluggish industrial economy. Hope and glory faded from the land, weakening both national and local fraternity. Internal tensions became more anxiously acute with economic stagnation, quickening inflation, and rising unemployment.

Meanwhile the trade unions, fostered by the further development of citizenship rights, had become more powerfully entrenched, more able to press sectional against national interest. As I argued in my fourth chapter, the incorporation of the Labour leadership both in Parliament and in the T.U.C., undermined the allegiance of the rank and file, reducing the 'governability' of those officially organized into the working-class movement.

There were also ideological movements in these post-war years with strongly divisive effects. The authority of churches and chapels declined still further. School teachers and parents became less effective conveyors of cultural values and traditional pieties as they too lost confidence in their right and their ability to be so. Scandals from the Profumo affair (1963) onwards dealt repeated blows to of course, total, even among its natural supporters—the Poulson revelations of widespread racketeering in the Labour strongholds of the North East were especially damaging to popular respect for the authority of both the Town Hall and Whitehall. There was a marked contrast between the moralistic Primitive Methodist Labour leaders, like Peter Lee, steeped in the proprieties of constitutional liberalism, and the political bosses like Dan Smith and Andrew Cunningham who replaced them, with their public relations networks and their eventual exposure and long gaol sentences for criminal behaviour in public office. And the adversary culture of students, intellectuals, journalists, and media men, grew more strident in the 1960s. The expansion of the univerities permitted the growth of social science, which emerged after 1965 as a powerful vehicle for radical criticism of established society. (Social science faculties in the expanding universities grew at three times the rate of the other faculties in the 1960s.)

Then, finally, came the sudden development of serious nationalism in Scotland, echoed by weaker but still significant separatism in Wales. Even the detachment of Northern Ireland became a possibility. These three countries, Scotland with 5½ million, Wales with 2¾ million, and Ulster with 1½ million population, are few in numbers compared with the 46 million who dwell in England. All four peoples are intermixed, geographically and by intermarriage, to a considerable degree, but are also to a greater or lesser degree opposed to the political and cultural dominance of the London metropolis. Minorities within them aspire to political independence and, in Ulster, social tension is further and tragically compounded by conflict between the Protestant majority and the one-third minority of Catholics who receive violent, if not wholly welcomed, support from the Irish Republican Army (I.R.A.) operating in part from Eire, south of the partition border.

In consequence, the United Kingdom faces an uncertain future, variously assessed and actively debated. One extreme, unrepresentative view which invites firm and urgent response is that it depends upon one's conception of the United Kingdom. There are those who believe that this rump of the former empire will last for ever, in an essentially unchanging evolution. Their number includes virtually all England, and a still formidable mass of allies in Scotland, Wales, and Northern Ireland. On the other hand stands the growing opposition—within sight of being a majority in Scotland—which accepts the verdict a great part of the outside world passed on Britain long ago: that it is a matter of time before it founders. Its post-empire crisis is long overdue, and not even to be regrettted. What else is likely to revive this polity of stultified anachronism and complacent privilege?[19]

8 Fraternity as citizenship

THE only way to meet the challenge of those who would dismiss any successful prospect for Britain is to turn from analysis of our present discontents to an attempt to chart the way to a brighter future. This does not mean abandoning objectivity. The determining of social ends should always be disciplined by study of the means to reach them: and that has been the burden of the earlier chapters. Exhortation alone is futile, whether to altruism or to tolerance or to recognition of the equal claim of others to share in the bounty afforded by society. The problem is to discover, to establish, and to strengthen those social institutions that will encourage and foster the kinds of relations between people that are desired.

I have asserted that liberty, equality, and fraternity are the three fundamental values in terms of which societies are to be judged. None of these ideals is fully realized in Britain. The question, then, is how each may be more fully realized. Simultaneous maximizing of them is not possible. It is a matter of finding the best balance between the revolutionary triad. Yet I believe that advance towards all three is possible, and that the limits of that advance depend upon the development of fraternal institutions.

But fraternal institutions is an ambiguous phrase. I mean it to denote social groups whose members share the same essential ideals of conduct—recognition of, and care for, the needs of others—which are associated with our noblest conception of the family. I take the notion of fraternity in political discourses to be a metaphorical reference to this ideal of a moral community, covering all the relationships, conjugal and consanguineous, that are entailed in the family. Indeed, it has sometimes been argued, and with force, that the fraternal metaphor impoverishes this conception: that brotherhood is more diluted and more prone to enmity than any of the other relationships; and that, in the revolutionary creed, 'brotherhood has been selected as the image of perfection, not because it represents the family at its best, but because it is the family at its least familial'.[1] Fraternity of this kind, in reality, rejects the family. But this is not my intention. On the contrary, while recognizing that family loyalties may limit or conflict with similar civic or community ties, I assume that the fraternal loyalty of the monk or the dedicated party member can and should be an overriding creed and code of conduct only for the the few. Nor is this type of human association a necessarily superior expression of moral integration. The ethical value of such a fraternity, whatever the self-sacrifice which it may entail, depends upon the treatment it gives to those who by choice or circumstance are not part of the brotherhood.

Moreover, just as the harmonious family, nuclear or extended, bears value in its own right, so too can the limited political community, even though it restricts itself to something less than the ecumenical brotherhood of man. The United Nations, the United Kingdom, England, Scotland, and Wales, can surely exist together. Of course, against those who advocate or allow particularistic forms of fraternity, the charge of 'contradiction' may be laid. Restricted definitions of community inevitably leave problems of external relations. Bounded human groups, by definition, always set such problems. But the proper reply, appealing to experience, is that the smaller group can cultivate the values to be applied in the larger. If these values are liberty and equality, then a practical meaning is given to the idea of the brotherhood of man. It is in this sense that I see fraternity, even though, and indeed because, it is rooted in small-scale organizations, as the pre-condition of liberty and equality. But, by the same token, the forms of fraternal association which can make up a fraternal society can vary, and communities can remain integrated while attaching different importance to liberty and equality.

Modern history has offered two contesting alternatives for realizing the revolutionary ideals—capitalism and communism. Western industrial capitalism pioneered the market as the central mediating institution in the development of wealth and its distribution. But the market promotes neither fraternity nor equality. It was historically the means of escape from feudal community and has been the target of Marxist criticism as the mechanism of class inequality and of the substantive restriction of liberty. Industrial communism substituted a state bureaucracy for the market. But here, and especially in the Russian case, the liberal critic can point to the repressive fraternity of the party which controls the State apparatus, and the sacrifice of political liberty in exchange for a far-from-perfect equality. Out of this contention the possibilities seem to be no more than a choice between two vast historical failures.

Is there another way? I think so. The third alternative, for Britain, is to take its own traditions of citizenship and democracy seriously in all their richness and inspiration. They offer the basis for a new fraternity without which both liberty and equality are impoverished. They offer also the political and social means of progress towards a newly-integrated society. They were pointed to in Durkheim's emphasis on local autonomy and respect for tradition in late nineteenth century Britain. They are best thought of as a *radical tradition*: a willingness to change institutions under changed circumstances so as to realize more perfectly the values sought by past reform.

The relevance of capitalism and communism, in any event, has to be put in the context of actual and present British circumstances. These, briefly recapitulated, are the legacy of a 'first-world' development, post-imperialism, tentative integration with the European continent, and centrifugal movements within the United Kingdom. But they also include a tradition of fraternity which has supported the slowly developing institutions of civic, political, and social citizenship. In Britain, political fraternity is citizenship. Its seeds were sown in the civil liberties of the seventeenth and eighteenth centuries. Its roots grew in the social inventiveness of the urban working class of the nine-teenth century, and in the traditions of public service which were developed by the liberal elements of the professional middle class. These have been the finest expressions of British membership one of another, but the Labour Move-ment has faltered in its attempt to nationalize the local welfare societies of an exploited class, and the ideal of public service has been diluted in its transformation to an over-powerful bureaucracy. So the political organization of citizenship, which is democracy, and the social organization of citizenship, which is community, continue to be thwarted by class interests and bureaucratic subversions.

What, then, are the prospects for a third way, through fraternity as citizenship, between the first and second worlds of capitalism and communism? There is no simple answer. The forces of conflict and cohesion are complex: and they stem from the wider world as well as from within our own society. Salvation lies neither in European integra-tion, nor in retreat to the more archaic native nationalism. These are conditions for successful solutions; they are not the solutions themselves. Nor is there any simple economic answer, whether through North Sea oil or a return to the market. Growth alleviates scarcity. But at our level of eco-nomic development, it stimulates appetite as much as it gratifies it. By fostering the positional good economy it lays up frustration as much as satisfaction.

Indeed, the greatest danger is precisely the offer of simple solutions to our complicated plight. We have an economy that does not release our energies, a polity that does not secure our trust, and a culture which does not sufficiently attract our affections. Simple solutions can only lead to political tyranny, whether from the Right or the Left. Either would destroy that fundamental element of our social life and tradition in which we can take pride—our long developed and tenaciously-held civil liberty. Our essen-tial predicament is that the historical conditions which allowed this liberty also permitted divisive inequalities of class and status, a stratified society held together by imperial might abroad and deference and respect for shared religious and cultural values at home. But external empire and internal social control have been losing their power to pacify without violence, leaving market success and political bureaucracy, in all their weaknesses, to justify a still markedly unequal society.

Past failures to achieve fair and equal social distribution have driven some to apathy, others to a belief in a violent seizure of power and the imposition of an authoritarian social order, and still others to denial of the possibility or even desirability of an egalitarian society. These are the roads to tyranny. Our experiences of industrial, nationalist, and racial conflict continually demonstrate the need for a new sense of equality to replace old class-restrictive liberties and status-crippled fraternities. We have still to provide a common experience of citizenship in childhood and old age, in work and play, and in health and sickness. We have still, in short, to develop a common culture to replace the divided cultures of class and status.

Our society cannot stand on such shifting foundations. To strengthen them, we need principles and practices of social distribution which are acknowledged to be just by the great majority. And in a world of growing visibility of reference groups, these principles will be seen as just only if they actually are just. The implication is that in a political democracy which secures our liberties, the paramount principle of distribution must be equality. Equality of opportunity is not enough. It is a state of affairs we have still not reached but which is, in any case, a step towards a society that could be more ruthlessly stratified than the one we live in now. Nor is it enough to eliminate all irrelevant discriminations of skin, colour, sex, cultural background, or family upbringing. We need full equality of the basic material conditions of social life. If poverty remains in Britain this is not because the technical means to its abolition are missing: it is because of an inadequate sense of moral implication in the lives of compatriots. It is a failure not of economic production, but of fraternal distribution.

The guarantee of the material essentials for freedom from want does not require even a radically-egalitarian policy. The fraternity nurtured in the kind of family experienced by the majority, extended by standards of schooling that most parents expect, and embodied in the political definitions of citizenship which were proclaimed during and after the Second World War, would put an end to poverty, once and for all.

Beyond this readily attainable minimum of a fraternal society, R. H. Tawney's conception still stands: Because men are men, social institutions—property rights, and the organization of industry, and the system of public health and education—should be planned, as far as is possible, to emphasize and strengthen, not the class differences which divide, but the common humanity which unites them.[2]

Unless they are shown to be relevant to needs, inequalities based on differences of personal quality are no argument against equality. Nor is the familiar argument that incentives necessitate inequality to be taken as a fundamental law of human economic nature. The incentives they assume are the products of present values and interests which arise from our existing institutions, and institutions can be changed. In a fraternal society it could reasonably be expected that any extra rewards to effort and capacity that might be necessary for an efficient division of labour would leave the basic structure of equal citizenship unimpaired.

The outstanding example of an established fraternal institution, one in which the most elevated familial ideal is extended voluntarily to the stranger, is the British blood donor system which R. M. Titmuss has compared with the marketing of blood in the United States and other countries to demonstrate that large-scale fraternity is a human practicality and not merely a Utopian exhortation. From his study of American practice, Titmuss concluded 'that the commercialization of blood and donor relationships represses the expression of altruism, evades the sense of community, lowers scientific standards, limits both personal and professional freedoms, sanctions the making of profits in hospitals and clinical laboratories, legalizes hostility between doctor and patient, subjects critical areas of medicine to the laws of the market place, places immense social cost on those least able to bear them—the poor, the sick, and the inept—increases the danger of unethical behaviour in various sectors of medical science and practice, and results in situations in which proportionately more blood is supplied by the poor, the unskilled, the unemployed, negroes, and other low-income categories of exploited human populations of high blood yielders.'[3] We do not have to assume with Titmuss that, in social institutions, there is a Gresham's law of ungenerosity. But we can recognize the opposite and integrating principle, which is to seek fraternity as citizenship in all public organizations. To do so is to encourage, through public policy, those fraternal motives which the blood transfusion service brilliantly exemplifies.

From this point of view there is nothing more important than the policy pursued by the State towards the family. Families have unequal shares of material and cultural capital. The remedy is positive discrimination. The material base for parenthood does not measure up to democratic standards of fairness. It is true that, no thanks to government, babies now tend to be born rather more in the better-off and less in the worse-off homes. Fertility is coming to be positively correlated with family income—a reversal of the previous absurdity. But mothers, and especially working-class mothers, are still at once the most hard-worked and the least-rewarded members of our working population. They are an essential element of the social division of labour but, unlike nurses, teachers, social workers and the like, are excluded from the paid occupational division of labour. They deserve an income which reflects their service to society. They deserve publicly-provided facilities in street child centres and play groups to relieve their isolated labours in raising the under-fives. The family is our best carrier of the basic education of each new generation of citizens. An enlightened social policy should recognize this and define the experts and specialist, the schools and the child services, as agents for the support, not the replacement, of family upbringing. The implication is that we must challenge the usurpation of authority by experts (whether they appear as teachers or as administrators) and grant full citizenship to the amateur parents against the professional pedagogues. This is what is meant, for instance, by the community school. Not parent governors as tokens in a ritual, but genuine parental and community government of schools.

In Chapter 6 I sketched the outline of an educational system giving balanced expression to the ideals of liberty and equality which would be a practical further development of the slow reform of the class-divided schooling bequeathed to Britain from liberal capitalism in the nineteenth century. The comprehensive primary and secondary school is its fraternal foundation, and could be the nursery of a fully democratic citizenship. The private market would have no place in it.

Political and industrial organizations could be refashioned to mirror the values cultivated in home and school. The twentieth-century trends in government and industry have made size and complexity into serious obstacles to effective citizenship and threaten to replace it by oligarchic and bureaucratic power. The increase of economic co-operation over larger areas makes all the more urgent the devolution of decision. Bold advances towards a more developed citizenship—in Scotland for the Scots, in the work place for workers, in the school for parents, in the locality for the neighbour, and so on, could evoke popular support. John Osmond's elequent plea for Welsh devolution, pointing to the way in which democracy should be rooted in community, is a persuasive contemporary example:

Man needs an anchor in a particular community. It is the source of that moral power which enables him to resist the monolithic State. The nation and the community in which he seeks his roots is not an end in itself: it is man's link with eternity. 'Cadw tŷ mewn cwmwl tystion', as Waldo Williams so movingly expressed it: man's relationship to the community is 'Keeping a home amidst a cloud of witnesses'.[4]

Similarly, economic organizations, with their characteristic legacy of hierarchy, increasing scale, low discretion, and low trust, could be re-directed towards industrial citizenship along the lines I indicated in Chapter 7.

These familial, educational, and industrial examples cover only a small part of the total range of the institutions of production and reproduction, all of which need to be measured and reformed in the direction which leads to a society which is integrated, because it rests on an optimal balance of what is possible to make real our traditional revolutionary dreams. My review of past progress makes it all too clear that the journey to a society of fraternal citizens is no easy one. Stratification is stubbornly resistant to change: there is bound to be opposition. There are always those who place private interest above public welfare. Yet in a society of the kind I am advocating, patient persuasion has to be our principal weapon: for persuasion is democracy in action. Only if it is given constant priority can we both guard our freedoms and override the resistance of vested interest. Only then, but certainly then, democracy has the right to enforce its will.

The attainment of a new and sound basis for social order requires political will of a strength we have hitherto lacked. No one can guarantee that either the challenge will be accepted, or the response forthcoming. But I would certainly claim that what I suggest we need is also socially and politically possible. Its elements are in our social traditions and on our political agenda. Adversity itself is now sufficient to give social response to political initiative. Here again the initiatives have to be congruent with the end in view: and that means democratic politics. Democratic politics is essentially a system in which citizens actively mould the final decisions binding on all. It works only if liberty of thought and expression is ranked first among rights and the active exercise of citizenship first among duties. Political action is inevitably carried on by imperfect people in public office. Hence the constant need for alert and knowledgeable citizens, to defeat oppression and to prevent the public services from degenerating into organizations which serve the private interests of public servants.[5]

That, all too briefly, is my view of our best way into the future. We have no paradise lost, no paradise to be regained. Yet we can, if we will, take heart from the ancient story of the departure of our primal ancestors from the Garden of Eden:

> Some natural tears they dropped, but wiped them soon;
> The world was all before them, where to choose
> Their place of rest, and Providence their guide:
> They hand in hand, with wand'ring steps and slow,
> Through Eden took their solitary way.[6]

Notes

CHAPTER 1

1 Joseph Peach Lehmann, *Remember You Are An Englishman: A Biography of Sir Harry Smith*, Jonathan Cape, 1977.

2 C. Crouch, *Class Conflict and the Industrial Relations Crisis*, Humanities Press, 1977, p. 3.

3 E. Gibbon, *The Decline and Fall of the Roman Empire*, J. M. Dent and Sons Ltd., Everyman edition, 1911-13, Vol. 1, p. 5.

4 (1735-1801). Professor of Civil Law at the University of Glasgow from 1761-1801.

5 (1723-90).Professor of Logic at the University of Glasgow from 1751. He then held the Chair of Moral Philosophy from 1751-63.

6 In *The Times*, 7 October, 1977.

7 W. Dibelius, *England*, Jonathan Cape (English edition), 1930. (First German edition 1922.)

8 ibid., p. 18.

9 T. Hobbes, *Leviathan*. Everyman edition, 1914, pp. 49-50.

10 M. Friedman, *Capitalism and Freedom*, University of Chicago Press, Chicago, 1962.

11 I. Berlin, *Four Essays on Liberty*, Oxford University Press, 1969.

12 R. Dahrendorf, *The New Liberty*, Routledge and Kegan Paul, 1975.

13 J. Rawls, *A Theory of Justice*, Oxford University Press, 1972.

14 R. H. Tawney, *The Acquisitive Society*, G. Bell & Sons Ltd., 1921. And *Equality*, Allen and Unwin, 1931, 4th revised edition, 1952.

15 F. Hirsch, *The Social Limits to Growth*, Harvard University Press, 1976.

16 ibid., p. 11.

17 Lord David Cecil, *The Cecils of Hatfield House*, Constable and Co., 1973, p. 267.

CHAPTER 2

1 This division of social organization derives from Max Weber. See H. Gerth and G. W. Mills, *Essays from Max Weber*, Kegan Paul, 1948, pp. 180-95. See also J. H. Goldthorpe and P. Bevan 'The Study of Social Stratification in Great Britain 1946-76', *Social Science Information*, 1977, vol. 16 (3/4), pp. 279-334.

2 See F. Parkin, *Class Inequality and Political Order*, Paladin, 1972 (first published by MacGibbon and Kee, 1971).

3 R. Dahrendorf, *Class and Class Conflict in Industrial Society*, Routledge and Kegan Paul, 1959.

4 For example, the Oxford Mobility Study, discussed briefly in Chapter 3 and more extensively in Chapter 6 below, has made a 36 and a 7-fold classification based on J. H. Goldthorpe and K. Hope, *The Social Grading of Occupations: A New Approach and Scale*, Oxford University Press, 1974. Note is also made below of the Registrar General's classification of five social classes (with a further division of Class III into its non-manual and manual components).

5 J. H. Goldthorpe and C. Llewellyn in their 'Class Mobility in Britain: Three Theses Examined', *Sociology*, Vol. 11, No. 2, pp. 257-87, May 1977. Table 2.1 is reproduced from this source.

6 See, for example, Daniel Bell, *The Coming of Post-Industrial Society*, Basic Books, Inc., 1973, Chapter 2.

7 R. Dahrendorf, 'Recent Changes in the Class Structure of European Societies', *Daedelus*, Winter, 1964, pp. 225-70.

8 Cf. Colin Clark, 'The Economics of Housework', *Bulletin of Oxford Institute of Statistics*, Vol. 20 (2), May 1955, pp. 205-11.

9 For details and guidance through the difficulties of measurement see A. H. Halsey, *Trends in British Society Since 1900*, Macmillan, 1972; and for later figures see *Social Trends*, a publication of the Government Statistical Service which is an invaluable source of material data on British social structures.

10 See *Social Trends*, No. 8, 1977, Table 11.2.

11 ibid., Section J.

12 J. Westergaard and H. Resler, *Class in a Capitalist Society: A Study of Contemporary Britain*, Heinemann, 1975, p. 43, use a figure of 30 per cent rather than 20 per cent. They are referring to 1960.

13 *Royal Commission on the Distribution of Income and Wealth*, Report No 5 (Third Report on the Standing Reference). Cmnd 6999, London, H.M.S.O., 1977.

14 See R. M. Titmuss, *Essays on the Welfare State*, Unwin University Books, 1958, pp. 34-55.

15 Westergaard and Resler, op. cit., p. 118.

16 ibid., p. 119.

17 J. B. Priestley, *English Journey*, Heinemann, 1934. Penguin edition, 1977, p. 296.

18 W. G. Runciman, *Relative Deprivation and Social Justice*, Routledge and Kegan Paul, 1966. Runciman uses the word power to mean what I refer to as party.

19 W. W. Daniel, *The P.E.P. Survey on Inflation*, P.E.P. Broadsheet 553, July 1975.

20 *Social Trends*, No. 8, 1977, Table 5.10.

CHAPTER 3

1 Published by Constable & Co. Ltd., 1935.

2 For an excellent short account see W. G. Runciman, op. cit., Chapter 5. See also R. M. Titmuss, *Problems of Social Policy*, H.M.S.O. and Longmans, 1950.

3 See G. D. H. Cole, *Studies in Class Structure*, Routledge and Kegan Paul, 1955, p. 65. His Chapter 3, 'The Social Structure of England', is a good brief summary of changes in the structures of class and status from the middle of the nineteenth to the middle of the twentieth century.

4 Robert Roberts, *The Classic Slum*. First published by the University of Manchester Press, 1971. Penguin edition, 1973 (to which my references apply).

5 ibid., p. 30.

6 ibid., pp. 160-1.

7 ibid., pp. 23-5.

8 Beatrice Webb, *My Apprenticeship*, Penguin edition, 1971, p. 171.

9 Richard Hoggart, *The Uses of Literacy*, Chatto and Windus, 1953.

10 See J. H. Goldthorpe and C. Llewellyn, loc. cit.

11 D. V. Glass (ed.), *Social Mobility in Britain*, Routledge and Kegan Paul, 1954.

12 G. D. H. Cole, op. cit., p. 58.

13 J. Westergaard and H. Resler, op. cit., pp. 324-33.

14 W. G. Runciman, op. cit., p. 96.

15 It is often assumed that Weber's conception of status is also trivialized by liberal writers who have identified it with the prestige of occupations. On this see F. Parkin, op. cit., pp. 29-32. But I think that the under-estimation of class in this tradition is the more fundamental error.

16 See T. H. Marshall, *Citizenship and Social Class*, Cambridge University Press, 1950. For a brief appreciation of Marshall, see D. Lockwood, *Sociology*, Vol. 8, No. 3, Sept. 1974, pp. 363-7. See also T. Geiger, *Society in the Melting Pot*, Kiepenheuer and Witch, German edition, 1950.

17 G. M. Trevelyan, *English Social History*, Longmans, Green and Co., 1944, p. 351 (quoted in T. H. Marshall, op. cit., p. 15).

18 T. H. Marshall, op. cit., p. 15. Marshall goes on to remark that the most celebrated actor in this drama was John Wilkes and, as he

puts it, 'although we may deplore the absence in him of those noble and saintly qualities which we should like to find in our national heroes, we cannot complain if the cause of liberty is sometimes championed by a libertine'. Perhaps Marshall was thinking particularly of the occasion when Wilkes was arraigned before a posse of outraged peers of the realm, one of whom declared, 'Wilkes, you will die on the gallows or of the pox': 'That depends, my Lord', Wilkes replied, 'on whether I embrace your principles or your mistress.'

19 This is made up of social security, £441; education, libraries, science, and arts, £314; health and personal social service, £281; housing, £195; environment services, £104; law, order, and protective services, £80; food and transport subsidies including concessionary fares, £45. (*Hansard*, 10 November, 1977, Written Answers, Column 186.)

20 *Social Trends*, No. 8, 1977. Table 3.15, p. 68.

21 ibid., Table 3.16, p. 68.

22 ibid., p. 69.

23 Michael Banton, *Race Relations*, Tavistock Publications, 1967.

24 E. J. B. Rose, *Colour and Citizenship: A Report on British Race Relations*, Oxford University Press, 1969.

25 J. H. Goldthorpe, 'Social Inequality and Social Integration in Modern Britain', in D. Wedderburn, *Poverty, Inequality, and Class Structure*, Cambridge University Press, 1974.

26 ibid., p. 221.

27 Barbara Wootton, *The Social Foundation of Wage Policy: A Study of Comparative British Wage and Salary Structure*. George Allen & Unwin, 1955.

28 *The Guardian*, 24 October 1977.

CHAPTER 4

1 See Colin Crouch (ed.), 'The Place of Participation in the Study of Politics', *British Political Sociology Year Book*, Vol. 3, *Participation in Politics*, 1977, Croom Helm, pp. 1-17.

2 S. E. Finer, *Anonymous Empire: A Study of the Lobby in Great Britain*, Pall Mall Press, second edition, 1961 (first edition 1958). See also J. D. Stewart, *British Pressure Groups: Their Role in Relation to the House of Commons*, Clarendon Press, 1958; and M. Kogan, *Educational Policy Making: a Study of Interest Groups and Parliament*, Allen and Unwin, 1975.

3 The relevant legislation was enacted in 1855-6.

4 Robert Price and George Sayers Bain, 'Union Growth Revisited: 1948-74 in Perspective'. *British Journal of Industrial Relations*, 1976, Vol. XIV, No. 3, pp. 339-55.

5 T. H. Marshall, op. cit.

6 Karl Marx, *Contribution to the Critique of Hegel's Philosophy of Right* (1844), in K. Marx and F. Engels, *On Religion*, Foreign Languages Publishing House, Moscow, 1957, p. 42.

7 Those juvenile thoughts, I appreciate, were neither humble nor meek.

8 A. Fox, 'Corporatism and Industrial Democracy: The Social Origins of Present Forms and Methods in Britain and Germany'. Paper prepared for the *International Industrial Democracy Conference*, July 1977 (Social Science Research Council), Cambridge, U.K. The papers will be published by the Social Science Research Council in 1978.

9 ibid.

10 See G. M. Young, *Stanley Baldwin*, Rupert Hart-Davis, 1952, pp. 93-4.

11 ibid., p. 95.

12 See R. T. McKenzie and A. Silver, *Angels in Marble: Working Class Conservatives in Urban England*, Heinemann Educational, 1968; E. A. Nordlinger, *The Working-Class Tories*, MacGibbon and Kee, 1967; W. G. Runciman, op. cit.; J. H. Goldthorpe et al, *The Affluent Worker*, 3 vols., C.U.P., 1968; F. Parkin, op. cit., 1971; B. Hindess, *The Decline of Working-Class Politics*, MacGibbon and Kee, 1971; R. D. Jessop, *Traditionalism, Conservatism, and British Political Culture*, George Allen & Unwin, 1974.

13 The Communist Party used to be described by Ernest Bevin as no less the enemy of the working class than the Tory Party.

14 D. Butler and D. Stokes, *Political Change in Britain*, Macmillan, second edition, 1974, p. 182.

15 P. Thorburn, 'Political Generations: The Case of Class and Party in Britain', *European Journal of Political Research*, 5, 1977, pp. 135-48.

16 B. S. Rowntree and G. R. Lavers, *Poverty and the Welfare State*, Longmans, 1951.

17 J. H. Goldthorpe *et al.*, *The Affluent Worker*, cited in note 12 above.

18 The *Report of the Committee on Financial Aid to Political Parties* (Chairman, Lord Houghton of Sowerby), Cmnd 6601, H.M.S.O. 1976, on the basis of replies from 91 constituency Labour Parties, estimated that individual membership by 1974 was down, not to two-thirds of a million, but to less than one-third of a million. The research organization, P.E.P., put the figure still lower at 250,000 (D. Leonard, *Paying For Party Politics*, London, P.E.P., 1975). In February 1977 the Gallup organization drew a representative sample of 315 local party organizations and asked the agent, secretary, or chairman to estimate the number of individual members in his own constituency Labour Party. Since the respondent's estimate was taken at its face value, the Gallup result is probably an over-estimate. Even so, in northern England, on these figures a full half of the constituency parties were reported to have 500 members or fewer, and only 12 per cent more than 1,000 members.

19 Dianne Hayter, *The Labour Party: Crisis and Prospects*, Fabian

Tract 451, Sept. 1977. In only 4 per cent of the Gallup constituencies
was the ratio of individual members of the Labour Party to Labour
voters better than 1 in 10. In half the seats it was worse than 1 in 30,
and it was worse than 1 in 30 in no less than 68 per cent of the constituencies in Labour-held seats in the Midlands, the North, and Scotland. The overall average was 1 to 26: the average for Labour-held
seats in the Midlands, the North, and Scotland was distinctly worse
at 1 to 35 (C. Martin and D. Martin, 'The Decline of Labour Party
Membership', *Political Quarterly*, Vol 48, No. 4, 1977, p. 464). By
1977 the inability of constituencies to finance them meant that
Labour had only 86 full-time agents, the fewest since 1946. About
half of the constituency parties were without youth branches in the
mid 1970s; even among the party members themselves who were in
the age range 15–25, only about 1 in 8 were members of the Young
Scoialists. (Labour Party National Executive Committee Report
1977, p. 20).

20 G. Tullock, *The Vote Motive: An Essay in the Economics of
Politics, with Applications to the British Economy*. Institute of Economic Affairs, London, 1976.

21 P. Johnson, 'Towards the Parasite State', *The New Statesman*,
August 1976.

22 Max Weber, *The Theory of Social And Economic Organization*,
translated by A. M. Henderson and T. Parsons, Oxford University
Press, New York, 1947, p. 337.

23 S. S. Wolin, *Politics and Vision: Continuity and Innovation in
Western Political Thought*, George Allen and Unwin, 1961.

24 ibid.

25 Quoted by Wolin, op. cit., from Lenin, *Selected Works*, Vol. 2,
pp. 447-8, 456.

26 R. H. S. Crossman, 'The Role of the Volunteer in a Modern
Social Service', in A. H. Halsey (ed.), *Traditions of Social Policy*,
Blackwells, 1976, p. 278.

27 N. Dennis, *People and Planning: The Sociology of Housing in
Sunderland*, Faber, 1970; *Public Participation and Planners' Blight*,
Faber, 1972.

28 R. H. S. Crossman, loc. cit., p. 268.

29 Robert Roberts, op. cit., p. 220.

30 David Caute, *The Fellow Travellers: A Postscript to the Enligh-
tenment*, Weidenfeld and Nicholson, 1973.

31 S. & B. Webb, *Soviet Communism: A New Civilisation*, 2 vols.,
Longmans Green & Co. First published 1935 (second edition 1937).

CHAPTER 5

1 D. Bell, *Toward the Year 2000—The Trajectory of an Idea*,
Beacon Press, 1969, p. 643.

2 M. Young and P. Willmott, *The Symmetrical Family*, Routledge and Kegan Paul, 1973, pp. 19 ff. For trenchant criticism of this view of economic growth, see F. Hirsch, op. cit., pp. 167 ff.

3 In a B.B.C. Third Programme Broadcast (1953), to which Lord Briggs kindly drew my attention.

4 R. Roberts, op. cit., p. 74n.

5 Arthur Waley, *The Analects of Confucius*, Allen and Unwin, 1938, p. 83.

6 E. R. Leach, *A Runaway World?*, B.B.C. Publications, 1968, p. 44.

7 Eleanor F. Rathbone, *The Disinherited Family*, Edward Arnold and Co., 1924, p. ix Introduction.

8 For a detailed analysis of the history of reduction of fertility in Britain, see Michael Teitelbaum, *The British Fertility Decline*, forthcoming.

9 These are graphically described by Lord Briggs in *Victorian Cities*, Odhams Press, 1963; Pelican edition, 1968.

10 See M. Teitelbaum, op. cit.; J. Habakkuk, *Population Growth and Economic Development Since 1750*, Leicester University Press, 1971; and J. A. Banks, *Prosperity and Parenthood: A Study of Family Planning among the Victorian Middle Classes*, Routledge and Kegan Paul, 1954.

11 A. H. Halsey (ed.), *Trends in British Society Since 1900*, Macmillan, 1972, Tables 2.36, 2.37, and 2.38.

12 J. Habakkuk, op. cit., p. 69.

13 See D. Pearce and M. Britton, 'The Decline in Births: Some Socio-economic Aspects', *Population Trends*, Vol. 7, Spring 1977, pp. 9-14.

14 Prepared by P. R. Cox for Young and Willmott, op. cit., Appendix 4.

15 F. Engels, *The Origin of the Family, Private Property, and the State*, 1884. Reprinted in Marx and Engels Selected Works, Vol. 2, Foreign Languages Publishing House, Moscow, 1951, p. 205.

16 R. M. Titmuss, 'The Position of Women' in *Essays on 'The Welfare State'*, George Allen and Unwin Ltd., 1958.

17 Eleanor F. Rathbone, op. cit., p. viii Introduction.

18 Margaret Wynn, *Family Policy*, Penguin, 1972.

19 Frank Field, Molly Meacher, and Chris Pond, *To Him Who Hath*, Penguin, 1977.

20 A. H. Halsey (ed.), *Trends in British Society Since 1900*, Macmillan, 1972, p. 118, Table 4.7.

21 *Social Trends*, No 8, 1977, H.M.S.O., 1977, p. 82, Table 5.3.

22 For a vivid description, see N. Dennis *et al.*, *Coal Is Our Life*, Eyre and Spottiswoods, 1956.

23 See J. H. Goldthorpe *et al.*, op. cit.

24 J. Cheetham, *Unwanted Pregnancy and Counselling*, Routledge and Kegan Paul, 1977, p. 2.

25 *Report of the Committee on One-Parent Families*, Cmnd. 5629, H.M.S.O., 1974. Chairman Sir Morris Finer.

26 *Social Trends*, No. 8, 1977, p. 116, Table 6.33.

27 Richard Hoggart, *The Uses of Literacy*, Chatto and Windus, 1957.

28 This, incidentally, is the basis for one interpretation of the student radicalism of the late 1960s, for example by Professor Edward Shils, 'Of Plenitude and Scarcity: The Anatomy of an International Cultural Crisis', *Encounter*, Vol. 32, No. 5, May 1969, pp. 37-57. They were the first totally-indulged generation, and recruited disproportionately from the better-off families most easily placed to create for their offspring the illusion of a world from which scarcity had been banished.

29 *Social Trends*, No. 8, 1977, p. 116, Table 6.33.

30 A. H. Halsey (ed.), *Educational Priority*, H.M.S.O., 1972.

31 Richard Hoggart, op. cit., p. 95.

CHAPTER 6

1 See D. V. Glass (ed.), *Social Mobility in Britain*, Routledge and Kegan Paul, 1954.

2 See J. H. Goldthorpe, *Social Mobility and Class Structure*, Oxford University Press, forthcoming.

3 Phyllis Thorburn, loc. cit.

4 The use of 'ten years after entry to the job market' as the 'destination' point had the advantage of standardizing the measure of mobility for each individual in the sample. It also may be expected to reflect the impact of education on mobility more clearly than a destination point which comes later in a man's working life. But this procedure yields a smaller amount of recorded movement into the middle class than is obtained by using 1972 occupation as the destination point. This is because the older men have a longer period in which to reach 'occupational Maturity' which, for this population, means greater proportions with middle and lower-middle class jobs.

5 J. H. Goldthorpe and C. Llewellyn, 'Class Mobility in Britain: Three Theses Examined', *Sociology*, Vol. 11, No. 2, pp. 257-87, May 1977.

6 G. Payne, 'The Lieutenant Class', *New Society*, Vol. 41, No. 772, July 1977, pp. 118-20.

7 See A. H. Halsey, 'Towards Meritocracy: The Case of Britain', in A. H. Halsey and J. Karabel (eds.), *Power and Ideology in Education*, Oxford University Press, New York, 1977.

8 See J. H. Goldthorpe and K. Hope, *The Social Grading of Occupations: A New Approach and Scale*, Oxford University Press, 1974.

9 J. H. Golthorpe, Clive Payne and C. Llewellyn, 'Trends in Class Mobility', June or September issue, *Sociology*, 1978.

10 The following summary relies on an unpublished draft of A. H. Halsey, Anthony Heath, and John Ridge, *Origins and Destinations*, Oxford University Press, forthcoming.

11 E Ashby and M. Anderson, *The Rise of the Student Estate in Britain*, Macmillan, 1970.

12 R. Dahrendorf, *The New Liberty*, Routledge and Kegan Paul, 1975.

13 J. K. Galbraith, *The New Industrial Estate*, Hamish Hamilton, 1967.

14 For a review of the current state of the debate on this issue see A. H. Halsey (ed.), *Heredity and Environment*, Methuen, 1977.

15 In his foreword to the first Newsom Report, *Half our Future: A Report of the Central Advisory Council for Education (England)*, Ministry of Education, 1963.

16 W. Morris, *News From Nowhere*, Thomas Nelson and Sons Ltd., 1890.

CHAPTER 7

1 See N. Glazer and D. P. Moynihan (eds.), *Ethnicity: Theory and Experience*, Harvard University Press, 1975.

2 On which see T. Nairn, *The Break-Up of Britain: Crisis and Neo-Nationalism*, New Left Books, 1977, pp. 82 ff.

3 D. Lockwood, 'For T. H. Marshall', *Sociology*, Vol. 8, No. 3, September 1974, pp. 363-7.

4 E. Durkheim, *The Division of Labour in Society*, translated by G. Simpson, Free Press, Glencoe, 1947.

5 Quoted by J. H. Goldthorpe in 'Social Inequality and Social Integration in Modern Britain', in D. Wedderburn, *Poverty, Inequality, and Class Structure*, Cambridge University Press, 1974, p. 232.

6 Barbara Wootton, *The Social Foundations of Wage Policy: A Study of Comparative British Wage and Salary Structure*, George Allen and Unwin, 1955, R. Dahrendorf, *Class and Class Conflict in Industrial Society*, Routledge and Kegan Paul, 1959; R. M. Titmuss, *The Gift Relationship: From Human Blood to Social Policy*, Allen and Unwin, 1970.

7 See, for example, Frank Parkin, op. cit., p. 49.

8 Kindly sent to me by Paul Cheetham.

9 A. Fox, *Beyond Contract: Work, Power and Trust Relations*, Faber & Faber, 1974.

10 T. Nairn, op. cit., p. 22.

11 See H. Perkin, *The Origins of Modern English Society 1780-1880*, Routledge and Kegan Paul, 1969, p. 187.

12 Herbert Asquith, 'The Volunteer', in *Poems of To-Day*, 2nd series, originally published separately 1922.

13 J. B. Priestley, *English Journey*, Heinemann, 1934 (Penguin edition 1977).

14 ibid., p. 65.

15 ibid., p. 126.

16 ibid., p. 127.

17 J. H. Goldthorpe, 'Social Inequality and Social Integration in Modern Britain', in D. Wedderburn, op. cit., p. 222.

18 See his *Relative Deprivation and Social Justice*.

19 T. Nairn, op. cit., p. 194.

CHAPTER 8

1 Ferdinand Mount, 'The Dilution of Fraternity', *Encounter*, Vol. XLVII, No. 4, October 1976, p. 20.

2 R. H. Tawney, *Equality*, Unwin Books, 1931 edition, p. 50.

3 R. M. Titmuss, *The Gift Relationship: From Human Blood to Social Policy*, George Allen & Unwin Ltd., 1971, p. 245-6.

4 John Osmond, *Creative Conflict:The Politics of Welsh Devolution*, Routledge and Kegan Paul, 1977, p. 251. Waldo Williams, 'Pa Beth Yw Dyn?' (What is Man?) in *Dail Pren* ('Leaves of a Tree'), Gwasg Gomer, 1956, p. 67. The quotation is in response to the question raised in the poem: Beth yw gwladgarwch? (What is a patriotism?). The poem is essentially about man's search for identity. 'Adnabod' (recognition) is only attained between man and man when the common root is discovered:

> Beth yw adnabod? Cael un gwraidd
> Dan y canghennau.
> (What is recognition? To find one root
> Beneath the branches.)

5 On this see Norman Dennis, 'Councillors, Officers and Public Participation', in Richard Rose (ed.), *The Management of Urban Change*, Sage Publications, London, 1974. See especially pp. 169-70: 'England has created for herself a civil service of municipal officers entirely subordinated to the popular will in law and in fact . . . The control of the expert by the amateur representing his fellow citizens is the key to the whole of our system of government.' When one considers that the literature of English local government, early and late, is full of such statements, it is apparent that, if councillors can be coped with and controlled with ease and with their acquiescence, there is little to be feared from participants with no *locus standi*, or whose *locus standi* is in no way comparable with that of the local government councillor. Indeed, from the point of view of 'correct' decisions being arrived at in the field of urban renewal, in so far as these lie within the jurisdiction of the English local authority, there is a great deal to be said for deflecting attention from the local government councillor. If he did not exist he would be regarded as an impossibly hopeful panacea, extravagantly Utopian, by exponents of 'power and the people'. His weaknesses and the weaknesses of his position are either shared by or exacerbated among any alternative contenders for influence on behalf of residents in areas of urban renewal. They have none of his strengths. While it is true, therefore, that officers are able to operate with a good deal of confidence on

the assumption that the 'correct' decision will be made by councillors, they can be even more confident that neighbourhood councils, residents' panels, and any other arrangement yet suggested which aspire to the councillor's functions without giving them the councillor's power, will also, save in the most exceptional circumstances, have their views accepted if they are 'correct', and if they are not, ignored. Like the roar going round Sunderland when Roker Park is full, the officers can chant in chorus: 'Easy! Easy!'.

6 John Milton, *Paradise Lost,* Book XII, ll. 645-9.

Further reading

GENERAL

To read more deeply into the subject of these lectures is a two-fold task. On the one hand it involves further study of theories derived from the social sciences, and on the other hand it calls for wider knowledge of the social, economic, and political history of Britain in the twentieth century. Relevant sources of social and political theory are mentioned in the suggestions for further reading under each chapter heading below. As a general introduction there is J. Plamanatz, *Man and Society*, 2 vols., 1963. On the side of historical sources, a compilation of social trends from the beginning of the twentieth century to the end of the 1960s is made in A. H. Halsey (ed.), *Trends in British Society Since 1900*, 1972. Then, from 1970, there is a convenient official source, *Social Trends*, published by the Central Statistical Office annually. This covers much the same ground as *Trends in British Society Since 1900* from 1951 and has added further 'social indicators' of particular interest in each year, for example, details of youth employment in the 1977 publication (No. 8).

Economic Trends is a companion publication, and B. R. Mitchell and P. Deane *Abstract of British Historical Statistics*, 1962, contains a useful long-run series. David Butler and Anne Sloman, *British Political Facts 1900-1975*, 1976, is a parallel and invaluable source of political information, now in its fourth edition and currently being revised.

There are bibliographies of work on British twentieth-century history in C. L. Mowat, *Britain between the Wars*, 1955, and *British History Since 1926: A Select Bibliography*, 1960, and A. J. P. Taylor, *English History 1914-1945*, 1966.

TO KNOW OURSELVES

Further reading on the study of society in general, and of British society in particular, could well begin with P. Cohen, *Modern Social Theory*, 1968, which offers a survey of contemporary sociological theory, and J. Rex, *Approaches to Sociology*, 1974, which is accurately described by its own sub-title as 'An Introduction to Major

Trends in British Sociology'. E. Butterworth and D. Weir, *The Sociology of Modern Britain*, 1970, is a more empirical introduction to the study of British society. K. Popper, *The Poverty of Historicism*, 1957, is the best modern book on methodology, and C. A. Moser and G. Kalton, *Survey Methods in Social Investigation*, 1971, the best introduction to survey methods.

The next step is to read more deeply into contemporary political argument. Brian Barry, *Political Argument*, 1965, is an excellent introduction. M. Friedman, *Capitalism and Freedom*, 1962, is a powerful exposition of libertarian theory. R. H. Tawney, *Equality*, 1952 edition, remains the best statement of egalitarianism, and R. M. Titmuss, *The Gift Relationship From Human Blood to Social Policy*, 1970, is an eloquent plea for fraternalism which might be read alongside Ivan Illich, *Tools for Conviviality*, 1973. Brian Barry, *The Liberal Theory of Justice*, 1973, is a good summary and criticism of John Rawls, *A Theory of Justice*, 1972. R. Dahrendorf, *The New Liberty*, 1975, is an excellent modern discussion of current social development from a liberal standpoint.

Finally, H. Gerth and C. W. Mills, *Essays from Max Weber*, 1948, and particularly Weber's essay on 'Class Status and Party' is an essential theoretical starting-point for the ground covered by the next three chapters.

A CLASS-RIDDEN PROSPERITY

A general introduction to sociological research and writing on stratification in Britain is provided by J. H. Goldthorpe and P. Bevan, 'The Study of Social Stratification in Great Britain 1946-76', *Social Science Information*, 16, 1977. Discussion of the general character of class in advanced societies is provided by A. Giddens, *The Class Structure of Advanced Societies*, 1973, and F. Parkin, *Class Inequality and Political Order*, 1972. W. G. Runciman's *Relative Deprivation and Social Justice*, 1966, is an important interpretation of the history of class and status in twentieth-century Britain in terms of the theory of relative deprivation. W. W. Daniel in his *The P.E.P. Survey on Inflation*, 1975, brings Runciman's 1962 survey up to date. J. Westergaard and H. Resler, *Class in a Capitalist Society*, 1975, presents a detailed account of British class structure from the Marxist standpoint. An outstanding empirical study of stratification in Britain is John Goldthorpe, David Lockwood, Frank Bechhofer, and Jennifer Platt, *The Affluent Worker*, 1968-9. All three volumes are relevant, Vol. 1, *Industrial Attitudes and Behaviour*, 1968, Vol. 2, *Political Attitudes and Behaviour*, 1968, and Vol 3, *The Affluent Worker in the Class Structure*, 1969.

For more detailed analysis of inequalities in income and wealth, there is H. Phelps-Brown, *The Inequality of Pay*, 1977, which uses data from many countries, and A. B. Atkinson, *The Economics of*

Inequality, 1975, which expounds the relevant methods of economic analysis. The most up-to-date information on the distribution of income and wealth in Britain is to be found in the Royal Commission on the Distribution of Income and Wealth (Chairman Lord Diamond) Report No 5, 1977. The reports of the Commission are continuing. Frank Field's *Unequal Britain*, 1974, is also useful, as are also the essays published in D. Wedderburn (ed.), *Poverty, Inequality, and Class Sturcture*, 1974.

THE RECONSTITUTION OF STATUS

There is no comprehensive modern study of status in British society. There are, however, useful studies of particular groups. Though very different in style, Richard Hoggart, *The Uses of Literacy*, 1957, and J. H. Goldthorpe et al, *The Affluent Worker in the Class Structure*, 1969, give authoritative accounts of the status aspects of working-class life in two different times and places. To these two works should be added R. Roberts, *The Classic Slum*, 1971, with its graphic description of status distinctions within a working-class district of Salford in the first quarter of the century. Two examples of status in more narrowly defined occupational groups are Norman Dennis et al, *Coal is our Life*, 1956, especially Chapter 5, and A. H. Halsey and M. Trow, *The British Academics*, 1971, Chapter 10. The status of coloured immigrants in Britain is well treated in the massive sociography by E. J. B. Rose, *Colour and Citizenship: A Report on British Race Relations*, 1969.

The essential source on citizenship as a special form of status is T. H. Marshall, *Citizenship and Social Class*, 1950, and his later work *Social Policy in the Twentieth Century*, 1967, should also be read. W. G. Runciman, *op. cit.*, contains the best general account of changes in status in Britain since the First War.

Reference is made in this chapter to the role of religion in maintaining the status system. For further reading on this question see D. Perman, *Change and the Churches*, 1977, and B. Wilson, *Contemporary Transformations of Religion*, 1976.

THE RISE OF PARTY

An illuminating introduction to British twentieth-century politics is S. Beer, *Modern British Politics*, 2nd edition 1969, placing politics in 'the age of organization'. The authoritative source on electoral history in Britain in the Twentieth century is D. Butler and D. Stokes, *Political Change in Britain*, 1974. C. Crouch, *Class Conflict and the Industrial Relations Crisis*, 1977, is a difficult but extremely worthwhile book on the relation between government and working-class organization. S. E. Finer, *Anonymous Empire: A Study of the Lobby in Great Britain*, revised edition 1966, is indispensable for the further study of 'party' as the term is used in this chapter.

The interpretation of organizational development in relation to the much debated idea of corporatism is well set out in J. T. Winkler, *The Coming Corporatism*, 1978, and well criticized in the papers collected together by the Centre for Studies in Social Policy, *The Corporate State—Reality or Myth?*, 1976.

Two studies of élite and power may be recommended: P. Stanworth and A. Giddens, *Elites and Power in British Society*, 1974, and W. Guttsman, *The British Political Elite*, 1963. Changes in working-class organization are discussed in B. Hindess, *The Decline of Working Class Politics*, 1971, and B. Jessop, *Traditionalism, Conservatism, and British Political Culture*, 1974. R. T. McKenzie and A. Silver, *Angels in Marble*, 1968, is a good historical study of working-class Conservatism.

BETWEEN THE GENERATIONS

Further exploration of this field might well begin with a general book on demography such as P. R. Cox, *Demography*, 4th edition, 1970. A good history of demographic development in Britain is H. J. Habakkuk, *Population and Economic Development Since 1750*, 1971, and the beginnings of the decline in fertility among the upper-middle-class Victorians are well studied in J. A. Banks, *Prosperity and Parenthood*, 1954. An excellent history of the evolution of the modern family in Europe and North America is Edward Shorter, *The Making of the Modern Family*, 1975. Two worthwhile empirical studies of the family in Britain are C. Rosser and C. G. Harris, *The Family and Social Change*, 1965, and M. Young and P. Willmott, *The Symmetrical Family*, 1973. G. Gorer's *Sex and Marriage in England Today*, 1971, is worth reading, and H. Gavron, *The Captive Wife*, 1966, is a well-known book on the role of the housewife. Childhood is well treated in J. Newsom and E. Newsom, *Four Years Old in an Urban Community*, 1968, and a modern treatment of the problems of family policy is M. Wynn, *Family Policy*, 1972.

MOBILITY AND EDUCATION

A recent survey and appraisal of the sociology of education may be found in J. Karabel and A. H. Halsey, *Power and Ideology in Education*, 1977, and an excellent textbook is O. Banks, *The Sociology of Education*, 1968. On meritocracy the indispensable source is M. Young, *The Rise of Meritocracy*, 1958. On comprehensive schools see C. Benn and B. Simon, *Half Way There*, 1972, and T. G. Monks, *Comprehensive Education in England and Wales*, 1968. The best historical treatment of the problem of equality in education is H. Silver, *Equal Opportunity in Education*, 1973, and an empirical study of educational disadvantage is A. H. Halsey, *Educational Priority*: Vol. 1: *E.P.A. Problems and Policies*, 1972.

The classic study of social mobility in Britain is D. V. Glass (ed.), *Social Mobility in Britain*, 1954. More recent work is reported in J. H. Goldthorpe and K. Hope, *The Social Grading of Occupations: A New Approach and Scale*, 1974, and in two forthcoming books from Oxford University Press, J. H. Goldthorpe, *Social Mobility and Class Structure*, and A. H. Halsey, A. F. Heath, and J. M. Ridge, *Origins and Destinations*.

THE BASIS OF SOCIAL ORDER

In the burgeoning literature on problems of devolution and disintegration in the United Kingdom, J. Osmond, *Creative Conflict: The Politics of Welsh Devolution*, 1977, is outstanding, but see also T. Nairn, *The Break-Up of Britain*, 1977, and C. Harvie, *Scotland and Nationalism*, 1977.

Criticism of the traditional British social order and proposals for its reform along egalitarian lines are to be found in R. H. Tawney, *Equality*, 1952 edition, and *The Acquisitive Society*, 1921. See also R. Williams, *Culture and Society*, 1959, and *The Long Revolution*, 1961.

For criticism of the basis of income distribution, a classic source is B. Wootton, *Social Foundations of Wages Policy*, 1955, but see also J. H. Goldthorpe in D. Wedderburn, *op. cit.*, 1974.

Analysis of the social order from a fraternitarian point of view is again R. M. Titmuss, *The Gift Relationship*, 1970, and also the essay by R. H. S. Crossman in A. H. Halsey (ed.), *Traditions of Social Policy*, 1976. A more general introduction to the study of social policy in Britain is Julia Parker, *Social Policy and Citizenship*, 1975.

A powerful study of social integration and anomie in the work place is A. Fox, *Beyond Contract: Work, Power and Trust Relations*, 1974. Norman Dennis's analysis of the relation between people, local government bureaucracies, and local politicians may be found in his *People and Planning*, 1970, and *Public Participation and Planners' Blight*, 1972.

Index